COMMUNICATING BY LETTER

MARILYN B. GILBERT
Praxis Corporation
New York, New York

John Wiley & Sons, Inc.
New York · London · Sydney · Toronto

Originally published as Letters That Mean Business

Library of Congress Cataloging in Publication Data

Gilbert, Marilyn B.
Communicating by letter.

(Wiley self-teaching guides)
Edition of 1973 published under title: Letters that mean business.
Includes index.
1. Commercial correspondence. 2. Letter-writing. I. Title.

HF5726.G55 1978 651.7'5 78-5999
ISBN 0-471-29897-2

Printed in the United States of America.

73 74 10 9 8 7 6 5 4

To the memory of my mother,

Rose Schotland Bender

Preface

Sooner or later, everyone has some reason to write a business letter. And almost everyone finds this difficult to do--even people who are normally comfortable with other kinds of writing assignments.

There are two good reasons why the business letter is a challenge. First, a business letter can have greater consequences than any other kind of writing. It can win a job or lose it. It can make a sale or sink it. It can clarify a puzzling point or obscure it further--and so on, over the range of effects from the most positive to the most negative. As everyone knows, a business letter *must* be right, and this obligation can be frightening.

Second, although many books claim to teach people how to write business letters, what they actually do is present specific samples from an infinite variety of business letters. Unfortunately, these books never provide a general plan by which all varieties of letters can be handled.

I hope I have succeeded in providing such a plan in *Communicating By Letter.* After analyzing thousands of business letters taken from the files of many different kinds of businesses, I found that all of these letters were written for one of three reasons: to *ask* for something, to *tell* something, or to *build good will*. And I found that we should follow the same general pattern whether we ask for a job, for information, for a particular favor, or for a hotel reservation. We should also follow the same general pattern whether we write to tell good news, to tell about a complaint, to tell about an adjustment, or to tell about a new product. Furthermore, we should vary the general pattern only slightly when we write letters of good will--whether we want to express congratulations or sympathy.

Once people learn a general plan they can apply to any kind of situation, they lose their fear of writing business letters, despite the big effect such letters can have. Readers of the earlier draft of *Letters That Mean Business* have reported that this was indeed true of them.

I am grateful for the help of many people: those business men and women who turned me loose in their correspondence files; friends who donated some sample letters that I used as models; reviewers who gave helpful comments and expert advice; and students who carefully read the exercises and answered the questions. I am also very grateful to Judy Wilson of John Wiley & Sons, Inc., for her most thoughtful criticism and suggestions.

As the sports columnists say, my family "deserves a lot of credit," and particularly my husband, Tom, who critiqued my materials. He has been extremely patient with me as I worked. Robby Gilbert and Eve Gilbert were very patient too. Thank you, Robby, and thank you, Eve.

Marilyn B. Gilbert

February 1973, 1978
New York, New York

How to Use This Book

Communicating By Letter is intended as a complete guide for producing any business letter or resume. However, you need not study each part of this book. Do you want to learn how to write letters, edit them, or type them? Whatever your goal, the following Chapter Guide should help you decide which sections of the book are relevant for you.

Other considerations, too, will help you decide how to proceed. You may be assigned to use Communicating By Letter as a textbook in a classroom; you may decide to use it on your own as a self-study course; or you may want to use it as a reference when the need arises. If you are going to use this book in a classroom, you will probably be asked to take both the preview and the review of each chapter you plan to study. (These previews and reviews are together at the end of the book in the section called FOR REFERENCE.) You are also encouraged to do these previews and reviews if you use this book on your own. If you are using the book as a reference, however, you would probably wish to skip the previews and the reviews.

Your answers on a preview will determine what you already know about the material to be covered. From this you can tell which parts of the chapter you would need to study and which parts you could merely skim lightly--perhaps skip altogether. If, for example, you should get everything right on a preview, you could skip ahead to the next chapter or read that particular chapter very lightly. If you miss everything on a preview, you would need to study everything in the chapter. After completing those parts of the chapter that you didn't know beforehand, you would take the review to measure what you have learned.

Looking through the book, you will find that each chapter is divided into numbered exercises, each followed by a dashed line. Answers or suggestions to any questions in the exercise appear directly below the dashed line. You should keep these answers covered, until you have completed your own answer. Then compare your work with the suggestions below the dashed line. If they are substantially the same, continue to the next exercise. If they are totally different, you should try to identify the problem and straighten it out before going ahead.

If you are using this book on the job as the need arises, you will find the section FOR REFERENCE most helpful--and particularly that portion containing Sample Letters. There is no virtue in struggling over every routine letter you have to write. If your letter is being written for the same purpose as that of a sample letter, you should use the sample letter and tailor it to your own needs.

Turn now to the Chapter Guide, and note that each chapter (sometimes each section) is described and labeled according to a function in the production of a letter. There is also a check-off column. You may check off what you feel will be relevant before you read any part of this book. In this way, your marked Chapter Guide becomes your course plan, and you can consult the Table of Contents for the specific pages you need. Another way to proceed is to check off each section after you have completed it. Beginning with the Introduction, your decision of which parts to study will be guided by what you have just read and by how well you are doing. With this method, the marked Chapter Guide becomes a plot of your progress.

Either mark your course plan now, or proceed directly to the Introduction, as you prefer.

Chapter Guide

Chapter Title	Teaches how to	Useful if you	Check (✓)
1. SETTING OFF IDEAS	give the appropriate stress to ideas by paragraphing the letter effectively.	write or edit letters	
2. ASKING LETTERS	write any letter whose primary purpose is to ask for something; this includes asking for a job, information, a reference, or payment on an overdue bill.	write letters.	
3. TELLING LETTERS	write any letter whose primary purpose is to tell something; this includes an announcement, a rejection, an apology, an adjustment, a complaint, a sales letter, a letter written for the record, or a letter to the editor.	write letters.	
4. BUILDING GOOD WILL	write any letter with the short-term objective of building good will; this includes an expression of thanks, regret, sympathy, or appreciation.	write or edit letters.	
5. SIMPLIFYING LETTER LANGUAGE	recognize outmoded expressions common to business letters and to find more acceptable substitutes.	write or edit letters.	

Chapter Title	Teaches how to	Useful if you	Check (✓)
6. TRIMMING THE HEDGE	treat the touchy situations: when to be direct in your writing and when to hedge, and how to use the language constructions that will enable you to do these effectively.	write or edit letters.	
7. ATTENDING TO DETAILS			
A. Copyediting for Common errors	detect any deficiencies in proofreading and lapses in grammar, punctuation, and usage.	write or edit or type letters.	
B. Expressing Numbers	express numbers in either of two common styles: figure style and word style.	write or edit or type letters.	
C. Dividing	divide a word at the end of a line so there is the least possible interruption to the reader.	edit or type letters.	
D. Typing a Neat Right-Hand Margin	use the typewriter bell as a clue that the margin line is approaching.	type letters.	
8. ATTENDING TO FORM	identify the parts of the letter, letter styles, and punctuation styles; also word the different parts of the letter to prevent any confusion about their meaning.	edit or type letters.	
9. WRITING YOUR RESUME	write a resume, or summary of your accomplishments, that will present your self and what you have done in the most favorable way.	are actively looking for a job.	

Contents

Introduction

Everyone always said that Mayor John Lindsay was really a Democrat at heart. At least he kept talking like one. But he kept doing Republican things, like nominating Spiro Agnew for Vice President in the 1968 Republican convention. Even some Republicans at heart wouldn't do that.

Then he began to do Democratic things, like risking open battle with New York Governor Nelson Rockefeller, losing the Republican primary for mayor, and winning the mayoralty on the Liberal party ticket. Why should he stay in the Republican party?

Between January 1 and April 17 of 1971, Mayor Lindsay received about a thousand letters from people all over the country inquiring about his political affiliation. This was the Mayor's form letter reply:

> Dear ________________:
>
> I recently received your letter concerning the subject of my party affiliation. I appreciate the concern you have shown.
>
> As you know, I am a registered Republican, and have no plans to alter my status. I hope to continue to speak out on the issues that face our cities and nation, from my position as Mayor.
>
> Thank you for taking the time and trouble to write.
>
> Sincerely,
>
> John V. Lindsay
> Mayor

Lindsay's letter exhibits the three characteristics of a good business letter: It is short in words; it is simple in style; and it is sincere in tone. And be careful if you're thinking it wasn't really sincere because Lindsay actually became a Democrat just a few months later. The tone was sincere--and that's all we can be concerned with here. (Mindreading is a different matter!) In fact, if we could find any fault with Lindsay's letter, it is that some of his expressions could have been simpler. For example, concerning the subject of could have been replaced by the single word about.

Another reason Lindsay's letter is good is that he wrote it to achieve a result: He wanted to thank the people who had written him--but without committing himself. All good business letters are alike in this: They are always written to achieve a result, even if this result is only to build a little good will.

Although this book is about business letters and how to write them, often there are other, better ways to communicate to get a desired action. A telephone call, for example, provides the opportunity for immediate discussion and an exchange of ideas. And would you believe that a long-distance call might even be cheaper? Always keep in mind that a letter takes someone's time to write and produce, and that a person's time costs money.

Sometimes a telegram is the best choice. It is certainly fast. But its key advantage is that it is very dramatic, and in some situations may be most effective for that reason alone.

A personal meeting is often better than the mail too, especially if its purpose is to settle a touchy matter. Written words offer no opportunity for a discussion, and they can leave a bitter aftertaste as a result. On the other hand, a lengthy meeting between well-paid participants costs a lot more money than many people realize.

These considerations are simple, and they are too often ignored. Enough bad letters are written every day to choke the files of respectable business offices. They are written and they are bad for the same reason: Nobody considered the possibility of using another way to communicate.

Just as an example, read the following real-life and very bad letter. (Only the names and the dates were changed, and for the obvious reasons.)

TO: Corporate Personnel

FROM: Vice President Ino Like

Subject: Annual Review of Mr. Heez Flatbeer

You will recall that Mr. Flatbeer's first annual review due in January 1972 was put off for

> months. As explained to you at that time, and to him, there was something about his performance which left us with uncertain and undefined but, nevertheless, very real doubts about where he would or could go in the department.
>
> This feeling of uncertainty has really not been dissipated even though his review in April 1972 supported an increase.
>
> Although called to his attention he is still almost invariably tardy and other work habits fall into this pattern also. The situation is being watched very closely.

Yes, it's too long; it has no style; and it sounds insincere. But, more important, it should not have been written in the first place. Either fire the guy or leave him alone; in any case, stop chipping away at him with pointless letters and memos.

To summarize, whenever you want to achieve a result by communicating, you must first decide which form of communication will work best. Should you send a telegram? Should you make a telephone call? Should you arrange a meeting? Or should you write a letter?

Here are some suggestions that may guide your decision:

(a) If time is urgent, make a phone call or send a telegram.
(b) If a dramatic effect is needed, send a telegram.
(c) If a discussion or an exchange of views is advisable, either telephone or arrange a meeting.
(d) If there is any chance the person might be offended by an impersonal letter, arrange a meeting or make a telephone call.
(e) If a record of some meeting or other situation is necessary, write a letter.
(f) If cost is a primary consideration, remember that a letter may not be the cheapest way to communicate: You must count the time the writer takes to compose the letter, the time the typist takes to produce it, and the time everyone takes to correct it. These activities may be much more costly than a phone call or a telegram, although a lot cheaper than a long meeting between well-paid people.

Let's apply these suggestions to an example. As you read the following situation, note the reason for a communication and look for special circumstances that will help you decide upon an appropriate form for communicating.

> SITUATION: Kathy Peters asks her friend, a literary agent, to read a short story she wrote. The understanding is that if the agent likes the story, he will try to sell it at the usual commission. But after reading the story, he decides it isn't saleable. He wants to communicate this message to Kathy in the gentlest way possible.

What result does the agent want to achieve? How should he communicate with Kathy to get that result? These are the two questions to ask yourself when you try to make a judgment about a situation that can be resolved by some form of communication.

In this case, the agent wants Kathy to know that her story isn't saleable, but he doesn't want to lose her as a friend. So, he probably ought to talk to her face to face, since this situation is a touchy matter. Assuming they live in the same city, a phone call doesn't show the same degree of attention, and a letter is downright cowardly.

Here is another situation that can be resolved by some form of communication. Decide what you would do:

> SITUATION: Markus Danby lives in New York. He hears of a job with a firm in Chicago, and he wants it. The man who does the hiring is an old friend.

Answer each question:

(a) What result does Mr. Danby want to achieve?__________________

____

(b) What form of communication would be appropriate?____________

____

____

(c) Why did you choose that form?__________________________

____

Now check your answers with the suggestions underneath the dashed line.

- - - - - - - - - - - - - -

(a) He wants the job.
(b) A telephone call or a telegram or a letter.
(c) You might have reasoned that a phone call is faster than the mail. But you might also have reasoned that a phone call would put Danby's

friend on the spot: Maybe he wouldn't want to hire Danby and also wouldn't want to turn him down. In that case, a telegram would give the friend the opportunity to think before replying. Or, if time is not critical here, a letter would serve the same purpose.

Situations like the two we've considered are typical. If a general principle applies, it is that you must weigh all relevant factors before deciding on the most suitable way to communicate.

As you know, the rest of this book is devoted to a later stage: The assumption is that the best way to achieve the results you want is to write letters--letters that ASK, letters that TELL, and letters that BUILD GOOD WILL. And you'll learn techniques for writing so these letters are short, simple, and sincere. (You'll also get some hints about writing effective telegrams in the section FOR REFERENCE.)

The first chapter is on paragraphing business letters. This, of course, is basic information for everyone who writes, edits, or types such letters. Continue now to Chapter 1.

CHAPTER ONE

Setting off Ideas

In speech we don't have paragraphs. Yet listeners are able to follow our shifts in thought because we give them clues--a change in tone of voice, a lift of an eyebrow, or a brief pause. We do this without thinking. If we occasionally dart from topic to topic without giving sufficient notice, our listeners cry "Halt!" and ask us to explain.

Not so in writing. The new paragraph is the clue to readers that something is going to change. And if we confuse things by failing to paragraph when we shift ideas, our readers can't stop us--they just stop reading what we've written.

If paragraphing is important to other kinds of writing, it is vital in a letter--since a letter is supposed to get results quickly. The paragraphs tell the reader what the writer wants him to do or know.

As an example, Sample A (below) and Sample B (that follows A) are identical except for the paragraphing. Which do you think is more effective?

(A)

Dear Mr. De Salvo:

Thank you for reordering Style 572. I plan to look after this order myself and send it out right away. Since I saw you last, we added another style that I think will work out equally well for you. One account that already tried it sold out in two days. I expect to leave for my next trip in about three weeks, and I hope to see you around the first of the month.

(B)

> Dear Mr. De Salvo:
>
> Thank you for reordering Style 572. I plan to look after this order myself and send it out right away.
>
> Since I saw you last, we added another style I think will work out equally well for you. One account that already tried it sold out in two days.
>
> I expect to leave for my next trip in about three weeks, and I hope to see you around the first of the month.

Don't you agree that Sample B is more effective? This letter is deceptive. It starts out by saying that one order was sent, but it next makes a sales pitch by describing a new product. Then it tells of plans for a visit. These three separate pieces of information go unnoticed in Sample A because they are not set off in separate paragraphs. More important, the sales pitch is buried--and the possible sale could be buried with it. In Sample B the three points are set off so the reader can easily respond to each one.

In this chapter you'll learn how to use paragraphing as a technique

(a) to separate points you want your reader to notice or respond to;
(b) to highlight a point; or
(c) to change the subject.

First you may want to work on the Preview to Chapter 1, which you will find on page 181. Most of the chapters have a similar preview of the main points that will be covered. From your performance on this preview you should be able to tell whether you can skim over the chapter lightly or whether you need to read it more carefully and do the exercises.

SEPARATING POINTS FOR A RESPONSE

1. You can make paragraphing pay off for you in any business letter.

One technique is to use a separate paragraph for each point you want your reader to notice or respond to. In other words, you can use physical layout to get your reader's attention. Of course, this means that a paragraph can be only a sentence or two. If you've learned somewhere that every paragraph must have at least four or five sentences, you may be wondering if this new advice contradicts your earlier training. It doesn't. The only strict rule about paragraphing is that a paragraph should be as long as it needs to be.

Using this technique of separating points may also mean that the subject will remain essentially unchanged from paragraph to paragraph. Again, this doesn't violate any paragraphing rules.

The following letter was intended only to build good will. In reading it, note how the paragraphing sets off each point John O'Day wanted Frank to notice.

Dear Frank,

(a) Congratulations on the promotion. This is one time the best man got the job!

(b) I hear you are now the boss of a brand-new computer--also the boss of the brand-new people who are supposed to run it. That sounds a lot like my job.

(c) Next month I plan to get to Chicago. Maybe we can get together. I'll call you.

Sincerely,

John O'Day

Describe the point of each paragraph in about three or four words:

(a) ____________________

(b) ____________________

____

(c) ____

Check your answers with the suggestions given below the dashed line.

Paragraph (a) expresses congratulations.
Paragraph (b) comments on the similarity of the jobs.
Paragraph (c) suggests they get together.

2. Proofreaders and copyeditors use a special symbol, ¶ , to point out where a new paragraph should start. It looks like a capital P for Paragraph. If you don't already use it, you should --because it's much more convenient than spelling out the word paragraph.

Here is a copy of a letter that the governor of Ohio sent to every Ohio voter and taxpayer, along with a booklet about the new state income tax. (Poor, neglected Ohioans never had to pay one before.) The copy of the governor's letter is exactly the same as the original except that the paragraphing was purposely left out. Even so, as you read this letter you will probably agree that the governor wanted the voters to respond to five points. To be sure of getting these responses, he signaled each point by making it a new paragraph.

Using these guidelines, see if you can put a ¶ at the beginning of each new point so the copy here will be paragraphed exactly the same as the governor's version:

FELLOW OHIOANS:

____(a) It is a great pleasure for me to introduce, to you the taxpayers, this booklet explaining Ohio's new tax structure. ____(b) It is our hope that this publication will enable you to understand all of the provisions of Ohio's important new tax law. ____(c) We hope it will answer the many questions you may have on this landmark legislation. ____(d) We believe Ohio's new tax structure is the fairest, most equitable program ever adopted in this state. ____(e) Should you have further questions, I urge you to contact the

Taxpayer Information Service of the Department of Taxation. ____(f) It is there to serve you, the taxpayers of Ohio. ____(g) Let me add a personal pledge. ____(h) I intend to see that every penny collected by the state under this new tax program is spent wisely and efficiently, and that every dollar we spend brings the greatest good to the largest number of Ohioans. ____(i) I believe the citizens of this state deserve no less.

Sincerely,

John J. Gilligan

Write a three-, or four-word description of the points the governor wanted the taxpayers of Ohio to notice in each paragraph. Identify each paragraph by the letter of the sentence that starts it.

Paragraph ( ):____

Paragraph ( ):____

Paragraph ( ):____

Paragraph ( ):____

Paragraph ( ):____

A ¶ sign could have been placed before sentences (a), (b), (d), (e), and (g).

Paragraph (a): Announcing the booklet
Paragraph (b): Booklet describes tax program
Paragraph (d): Governor praises tax program
Paragraph (e): Where to get questions answered
Paragraph (g): Governor's pledge for honest spending

3. This kooky letter (written by our old friend Anonymous) makes the round of large business offices all over the country. Of course, it's just a spoof of the stuffy language and senseless subject matter of office memos that waste office workers' eyesight. But it is included here because it also offers paragraphing practice.

Put a ¶ in front of each sentence that you think should begin a new paragraph:

TO: All Office Personnel

Subject: New Sick Leave Policy

____(a) It has been brought to our attention that the attendance record of the employees at the Sporlan Valve is a disgrace to our gracious benefactors, who at present have given you a job. ____(b) Due to the lack of consideration for your job with so fine an organization, as shown by such frequent absenteeism, it has become necessary for us to review some of our policies and put some changes into effect. ____(c) Sickness is no excuse. ____(d) We will no longer accept your doctor's statement as proof, as we believe that if you are able to go to the doctor, you are able to come to work. ____(e) Death (other than your own) is no excuse. ____(f) There is nothing you can do for the dead, and we are sure that someone else with a lesser position can attend to the arrangements. ____(g) However, if the funeral can be held in the late afternoon, we will be glad to let you off one hour early, provided that your share of the work is ahead enough to keep the job going in your absence.

____(h) About a leave of absence for an operation, we believe as long as you are an employee here you will need all the strength you have, and should not consider having anything removed. ____(i) We hired you as you are, and to have anything removed would certainly make you less than what we bargained for. ____(j) Death--your own--will be accepted as an excuse.

____(k) But we would like two weeks' notice, as we feel it's your duty to teach someone your job.

THANK YOU FOR YOUR ATTENTION,

THE MANAGEMENT

Check your paragraphing with the suggested answers.

A ¶ sign could have been placed before sentences (a), (c), (e), (h), and (k). Each paragraph covers a separate point that the reader should notice.

HIGHLIGHTING A POINT

4. A second paragraphing technique is to highlight a point by setting off the single sentence that expresses it.

Notice that the letter that follows wasn't paragraphed. After you've read it through, you will probably agree that it really doesn't need to be.

But suppose you wanted to emphasize the number of reminders you have already sent. Remember that you can highlight the single sentence that expresses this point by setting it off in a paragraph by itself. Use the ¶ to do this now:

Dear Mr. Detts:

____(a) You have probably overlooked our last invoices. ____(b) Or maybe they didn't reach the right person in your company. ____(c) Whatever the reason, this is the third reminder! ____(d) We know you understand the importance of keeping your credit in order. ____(e) So, we hope to receive your check in the next few days.

A ¶ could have been placed before sentences (a), (c), and (d). Notice the difference the paragraphing makes.

(a) You have probably overlooked our last invoices. (b) Or maybe they didn't reach the right person in your company.

(c) Whatever the reason, this is the third reminder!

(d) We know you understand the importance of keeping your credit in order. (e) So, we hope to receive your check in the next few days.

CHANGING THE SUBJECT

5. As you know, there is no right or wrong way to paragraph a letter, just as there is no right or wrong way to paragraph any other kind of writing.

However, the third technique of paragraphing is one you have probably heard and applied so often that you regard it as a rule: Start a new paragraph when you want to change the subject.

In the previous exercise you noted the effect of highlighting a single message. Look over the same letter again. This time, try to suggest an alternative paragraphing arrangement based on the practice of starting a new subject with a new paragraph. (Use the ¶ .)

> Dear Mr. Detts:
>
> ____(a) You have probably overlooked our last invoices. ____(b) Or maybe they didn't reach the right person in your company. ____(c) Whatever the reason, this is the third reminder. ____(d) We know you understand the importance of keeping your credit in order. ____(e) So, we hope to get your check in the next few days.

One possibility is for sentence (a) to start the first paragraph and sentence (d) to start the second. By doing this, you divide the letter into the past history of the overdue account and the need for saving a credit rating.

A second possibility is for sentence (a) to start one paragraph and sentence (c) to start another. Now the subject changes from an account of what happened in the past to recommendations for the present.

APPLYING ALL PARAGRAPHING TECHNIQUES

6. The memo on the following page can be paragraphed in several ways. Read it first, looking for alternatives.

TO: Holgate Division

FROM: Gale Force, Manager

Subject: Feeding the Coffee Machine

(a) How quickly we forget! (b) Remember how enthusiastic we were about the coffee machine? (c) Coffee would be ready any time we wanted it, and not just twice a day when the coffee vendor remembered us. (d) We would pay just 10 cents a cup instead of the 27 cents the coffee vendor asks for. (e) Unfortunately, the coffee machine isn't paying its way these days. (f) And if the situation doesn't improve, we'll have to throw ourselves on the mercy of the coffee vendor once more. (g) So, please help keep us in continuous coffee by remembering to put 10 cents in the tin each time you "Draw One."

Write the numbers of the sentences that begin new paragraphs for each alternative paragraphing suggestion:

Suggestion 1: ______________

Suggestion 2: ______________

Four alternative paragraphing suggestions are given below the dashed line. You should have written at least two of them. And if so, you may continue to the Review of Chapter 1, which you will find on page 182. Then continue to Chapter 2 to learn how to write Asking letters--that is, letters that ask for anything from a job to the price of Campbell's chicken soup in Caracas. If you're interested in editing letters or setting them up for type, but not in actually writing them, consult the Chapter Guide to see where to go next.

Suggestion 1: (a), (b), (e)
Suggestion 2: (a), (e), (g)
Suggestion 3: (a), (e)
Suggestion 4: (a), (b), (e), (g)

CHAPTER TWO
Asking Letters

Read this letter addressed to Professor Persky, a professor of education at the state university, and decide how you would respond to it.

Dear Professor Persky:

I belong to a woman's club that meets once a month to discuss timely topics and good books. Most of us are mothers in our thirties or forties, and are well educated though inexperienced in the ways of the world. We're concerned about ecology, for example, but don't know what we can do to help protect our environment. We're concerned about crime in our cities, but are not sure that using more policemen will solve the problem. And we read books that the major book clubs promote, like Eleanor and Franklin and John Updike's novels.

At our last meeting, we agreed that we would like to ponder your views on education. As the program chairman, I was asked to write to you. Would you come speak to our little group?

Please let me know your answer immediately so I can make the necessary arrangements. I thank you in advance.

Very truly yours,
Bertha Bennett
Bertha Bennett, Program Chairman
(Mrs. Clarence Bennett)

Professor Persky might well have responded like this: "You want my views on your education? I think you need to learn how to write a simple request first. What would you like me to talk about? Ecology? President Roosevelt? Education is a lifetime process. What aspect of this process do you want me to discuss? When? Where? And you shouldn't have thanked me in advance, because the answer to whatever you're asking me to do is a firm "No."

Bertha Bennett's letter failed because she introduced details before she got to the point--which, by the way, was none too clear. Furthermore, her ending was brusque in a letter whose purpose was to ask a favor.

Yet, with just a few rearrangements and other changes, Bertha Bennett might have written this successful letter:

194 Henry Street
Hopewell, Pennsylvania 70412
October 4, 1973

Dear Professor Persky:

The Gettysburg Women's Cultural Club would like you to speak at our November 14 meeting on the plight of the high school dropout. We will use the auditorium in the main library building from 2:00 to 4:00 p.m.

Perhaps you should know more about us. We meet once a month to discuss timely topics and good books. Most of us are mothers in our thirties or forties, and are well educated though inexperienced in the ways of the world. We're concerned about ecology, for example, but don't know what we can do to help protect the environment. We're concerned about crime in the cities, but are not sure that having more policemen will solve the problem. And we read books that the major book clubs promote, like Eleanor and Franklin and John Updike's novels.

I hope you can accept our invitation. You may either write me at the address above, or call me at 377-3768.

Very truly yours,
Bertha Bennett
Bertha Bennett, Program Chairman
(Mrs. Clarence Bennett)

There is no guarantee that Professor Persky will accept this invitation either. But now Mrs. Bennett's letter does state its purpose right away so the Professor knows what she wants; it gives complete details that will help him reach his decision; and it ends by making it easy for him to respond.

This chapter covers all letter-writing situations in which the primary purpose is to ask for something: a job, some information, some kind of merchandise, a reference for a bill or for credit, or a payment on an overdue bill. The situations here cover everyday topics. But from time to time you may need to make requests of professionals and businessmen who use special technical terms that may obscure very simple concepts. You may use the Glossary of Selected Business Terms (on page 244) to find out what these unfamiliar words and expressions mean.

First, you may want to work on the Preview to Chapter 2, which you will find on page 184.

PATTERN OF AN ASKING LETTER

1. Whenever you write a letter Asking for something, you of course want it to get favorable attention and bring a satisfactory result. To make success most likely, you should follow three steps:

(a) In the first paragraph--maybe even in the first sentence--you should say why you're writing. If possible, you can refer to previous correspondence or to phone calls--anything that will help acquaint your reader with the situation. This step is the so-called Orientation.

(b) Next, you should state whatever Information the reader would need in order to supply what you've asked for. If the request is very simple, you might put the Information and the Orientation in the same paragraph--maybe even in the first sentence. But if the Information is detailed, you can put it in a separate paragraph or paragraphs.

(c) In the last paragraph, you should state what Action you want the reader to take. Even in a short letter, you probably should set the Action off in a paragraph by itself so the reader can respond to it easily. If you know the reader, you may also want to make a personal Addition.

Overall your letter must be short, simple, and sincere.

If you follow these steps, you will set things up so you are most likely to get the results you want. But keep in mind that this pattern is only a guide. Special situations would demand some special twists. You should always keep your eye on your goal and on how best to achieve it.

Read this example of an Asking letter, to note how it follows the general pattern.

Dear Mr. Ruckinski:

(a) I am answering your advertisement in the July 16 issue of The Indianapolis Star for a proofreader.

> (b) My resume* is enclosed. If you like, I will give you names of references to call. But I hope you will consider this application confidential and not contact my present employer.
>
> (c) If you would like to interview me, I can arrange to take the time off.

You might change some of the words, but you will probably agree that this letter follows the prescribed pattern for an Asking letter.

Briefly (in about three or four words) describe what each paragraph achieves:

(a) ____

(b) ____

(c) ____

Paragraph (a) explains the reason for the letter.
Paragraph (b) explains where to find out more about the applicant.
Paragraph (c) suggests what action the reader might take.

2. So, an Asking letter generally follows this sequence:

(a) It starts off by explaining the reason for writing.
(b) Next, it gives enough details to enable the reader to satisfy the request.
(c) Last, it makes the request--asks the reader to take an Action.

Remember, for convenience, we call these parts (a) Orientation, (b) Information, and (c) Action. And keep in mind that a personal Addition may be included if the reader is a friend or acquaintance.

In the letter in the previous exercise, these three main parts were expanded into three separate paragraphs. But, as you know, some Asking letters are so brief that we can handle the first two essentials

*A resume is a summary of job qualifications--a self-description--which you may send with a letter Asking for a job. You can find out how to write a resume in Chapter 9.

in one paragraph (sometimes in only one sentence!) and then make the Action a paragraph by itself so it will get the attention it needs.

Note in the letter below that sentence (a) takes care of the Orientation and most of the Information, and that sentence (b) gives the remaining detail. Now, start a new paragraph, and write an Action that requests confirmation of the reservation.

Gentlemen:

(a) Please reserve a cabana room with a double bed for my wife and me on August 16. (b) We expect to check in by 1:30 p.m.

(c) ____

____

Very truly yours,
Norman Barrows
Norman Barrows

(c) Can you confirm our reservation by August 12?
(A period after 12 would be equally acceptable to most people. However, there are some who would regard a request followed by a period as a command and therefore not nearly so polite.)

MAKING MORE THAN ONE REQUEST

3. An Asking letter--even a very brief one--may make more than one request. If so, we can make sure the reader notices each request by setting it off in a paragraph by itself, as in the following sample.

Gentlemen:

(a) Please reserve a cabana room with a double bed for my wife and me on August 16.

(b) Can you confirm our reservation by August 12?

(c) I'm worried about transportation from El Paso to Juarez. Our flight is No. 884, which arrives in El Paso at 12:55.

(d) Can you send a taxi to meet us?

Very truly yours,
Norman Barrows
Norman Barrows

This setup should bring two answers. As you see, each request has its own Orientation and its own Information.

Sometimes you'll want to handle each request separately, as in the letter here; and sometimes you'll want to vary the pattern. One variation is to combine Orientations for both requests, then combine Information, and last state each Action in a separate paragraph. Other variations may work out well too.

Now suppose Norman Barrows wants to add still one more request to his letter: He explains that he and his wife are bringing their baby, and he asks if they can have a crib in the room.

(a) Rewrite the first paragraph to include the Orientation for this third request: ____________________

____

(b) Write the Action for the third request: ____________________

____

(c) Where would you add this third Action? ____________________

____

(d) This time, write the Action and Orientation for this third request together in one sentence: ________________________________

____

(e) Where would you add this sentence? ________________________

- - - - - - - - - - - - - - -

(a) Please reserve a cabana room with a double bed for my wife and me on August 16. We're bringing our baby too.
(b) Could we have a crib in our room?
(c) Probably after paragraph (b)
(d) Could we have a crib in our room for our baby who will be traveling with us?
(e) Probably after paragraph (d)

WRITING AN ORIENTATION

4. To summarize, you write an Asking letter when you want something: a job, information, a reservation, an appointment, a reference, and so on. You are most likely to get a response by following the general pattern of presenting an Orientation to the request first; Information supporting this request next; and the Action at the end--preferably in a separate paragraph. If you make more than one request in the Asking letter, you have to adjust this pattern somewhat to include Orientation to each request and any necessary information.

The rest of this chapter offers practice in writing the major parts of an Asking letter. In each exercise, you'll be asked to read a situation or situations that can be resolved by an Asking letter. The strategy is to put yourself in the reader's place, if possible, and decide what would make the biggest impact on him.

First, the Orientations. Read this situation. If you don't know what some of the words mean, look them up in the Glossary of Selected Business Terms, page 244.)

> SITUATION: Assume that you are freelance writer Janet Dugan. The Internal Revenue Service has audited your tax return and is questioning the cost of a move you made from Atlanta to New York on December 21 and deducted as a business expense. You need the bill of lading as the proof. So, you request this from the Suddath Moving Company in Atlanta.

An Orientation to an Asking letter that would resolve this situation might be as follows:

> On my federal income tax last year, I deducted the cost of a move your company made for me since it was a business expense. However, the Internal Revenue Service has asked me for the bill of lading as proof.

This Orientation is satisfactory, but maybe not the most effective one. The words Internal Revenue Service make everyone jump, and the people in the moving company would not be an exception. Try writing another Orientation to this situation--this time, by starting off with IRS.

The Internal Revenue Service has asked me to send a bill of lading as proof of a move that your company handled for me, since I deducted it as a business expense on my income tax return.

OR

The Internal Revenue Service has asked for a bill of lading as proof of a move your company handled for me.

5. For practice, Write an Orientation for each of these situations.

SITUATION (a): You saw an advertisement in the March issue of the House and Garden magazine for an electric appliance that makes yogurt. You want to order one. But since you have misplaced the March issue, you must write directly to the magazine for ordering information. You do recall that you should order from the store nearest you. You live in Cleveland.

ORIENTATION (a):

SITUATION (b): Your boss is writing a book to be published by John Wiley & Sons. He wants to use paragraph 2 on page 32 of Writers at Work, Volume III, which was published by Viking Press in 1967. He wants you to write Viking for permission to quote. He will sign the letter.

ORIENTATION (b):

- - - - - - - - - - - - - -

(a) I would like to order one of those yogurt makers you advertised in your March issue.
(b) I would like to quote from a Viking book in a manuscript that I am preparing for John Wiley & Sons.

WRITING THE INFORMATION

6. You'll find the second part of the Asking letter--the Information--simple to write once you have already written an effective Orientation. But keep in mind that you must include every detail that your reader would need so he can respond to the request--and nothing more. In fact, any information that isn't absolutely essential could interfere with the primary objective of getting an appropriate response.

Let's look again at the first situation about the request for a bill of lading and consider what sorts of things would be appropriate for the Information. (The situation is repeated in case you forgot the details.)

> SITUATION: Assume that you are freelance writer Janet Dugan. The Internal Revenue Service has audited your tax return and is questioning the cost of a move you made from Atlanta to New York on December 21 and deducted as a business expense. You need the bill of lading as the proof. So, you request a copy of this document from the Suddath Moving Company in Atlanta.

You reason that Suddath keeps its records by name or date and perhaps both. You of course need to include this information and also the destination. So, the Information portion of this letter might be as follows:

> INFORMATION: As your records will show, the Suddath Moving Company moved Janet Dugan from Atlanta to New York City on December 21, 1971.

You could tack this information onto the Orientation in the first paragraph, or you could set it off by itself--as you like it.

But, can you think of any reason why you might want to set off the Information here by itself?______________________________

____

- - - - - - - - - - - - - -

A separate paragraph might help the clerk in the Suddath Moving Company check the Company's records against your facts.

7. Now see if you can Write the Information parts of Asking letters to follow the Orientations you have already written. The situations are repeated here in case you have forgotten the details. (You will probably want to refer to your own Orientations too.)

SITUATION (a): You saw an advertisement in the March issue of the House and Garden magazine for an electric appliance that makes yogurt. You want to order one. But since you have misplaced the March issue, you must write directly to the magazine for ordering information. You do recall that you should order from the store nearest you. You live in Cleveland.

INFORMATION (a):

SITUATION (b): Your boss is writing a book to be published by John Wiley & Sons. He wants to use paragraph 2 on page 32 of Writers at Work, Volume III, which was published by Viking Press in 1967. He wants you to write Viking for permission to quote. He will sign the letter.

INFORMATION (b):

\- - - - - - - - - - - - - - -

(a) Unfortunately, I have misplaced my March issue. But I do recall that I can order from the nearest store. As you see, I live in Cleveland. (You might either tack this on to the first paragraph or set it off by itself--as you prefer.)
(b) The passage I'd like to use is the second paragraph on page 32 of Writers at Work, Vol. III, which was published in 1967.

[Again, you might either tack this Information onto the first paragraph or set it off by itself. Another possible treatment for this situation is to write Orientation and Information together in one sentence, as here for example: I would like to quote the second paragraph on page 32 of Writers at Work, Vol. III (published in 1967), in a manuscript that I am preparing for John Wiley & Sons.]

WRITING THE ACTION

8. And now the Action.

For the sample situation in which you want the bill of lading as proof of the cost of a move from Atlanta to New York, you might wind up with this statement of Action:

> Would you please send me a copy of the bill of lading? I have enclosed a self-addressed envelope.

Although you don't need to mention it, the self-addressed envelope should of course be stamped. The self-addressed, stamped envelope is a device that helps to ensure a speedy reply. It may also be necessary for getting any reply. Many people who write articles in professional journals, for example, will not furnish a reprint unless a stamped, self-addressed envelope accompanies the Asking letter. Always keep in mind that the reader is more likely to act if you make everything as easy as possible for him to do so.

One trap to avoid, however, is the temptation of the half sentence "Thanking you in advance" or its cousins. This is trite. More important, it could also be construed as impolite, even though it may have been intended as a courtesy. Remember, you cannot presume that the reader will give you what you want; you must let him make up his own mind.

In short, you should keep your please's and your thank you's straight. If you are really grateful--or will be if he responds as you asked--you can thank him later in a separate letter. (See Chapter 4, BUILDING GOOD WILL.)

Many people tack on a "Thanking you in advance" to a request for no other reason except that they have read it so often that a letter sounds abrupt without it. But this is foolish. Keep in mind that a business letter should be long enough to achieve its purpose--and then it should stop. Of course, if you know the person you are writing to, you may want to add a personal comment (an Addition) after you state the Action.

Write a suitable Action for the two situations we've been dealing with. (Look back to the previous exercises to recall the situations. Also, review the Orientations and Informations that you wrote.)

ACTION (a):

ACTION (b):

(a) Please give me the necessary ordering information. I have enclosed a self-addressed envelope.
(b) May I have your permission to do this? I have enclosed a self-addressed envelope.

WRITING ALL THREE PARTS

9. In this exercise, you'll write a complete Asking letter to resolve a "collection" situation. If you've ever been in debt yourself, you'll agree that creditors make use of many strategies in Asking for their money.

Department stores, for example, send a series of letters in ever-increasing degrees of severity. First the notice asks politely for payment; it also implies faith in the debtor's ability to pay by suggesting that he continue to shop and to enjoy the store's many bargains.

If the debtor fails to respond to this notice, the next letter is more stern: It's still polite, but it no longer encourages further shopping. After this, there might be a firm yet polite threat (if a threat can be polite) to refer the matter to a collection agency. Threats may continue for a long time before the matter is actually turned over to a professional money collector.

We won't cover the technique of writing collection letters in any detail in this book. Large companies who use the harsher-and-harsher approach usually have form letters anyway. But there are occasions when you do need to ask for money that is owed to you personally or to your company, and form letters are not relevant. Here, you can follow the same principles that would guide you in asking for anything else.

Read the situation, and then write an Asking letter that you hope will resolve it:

> SITUATION: You're an artist. In July 1972 you illustrated a book for an author of children's books--a Clem Magee. Mr. Magee promised to pay you $500. So far, he has paid only $100. (He paid this in January 1972.)

Dear Mr. Magee:

As you will recall, you still owe me $400. After I illustrated your book in July 1972, you promised to pay me $500. So far, however, you have paid me only $100. This was in January 1972.

I have enclosed a self-addressed envelope. Won't you please use it to send me the remaining $400?

(Another possibility is to set the first sentence off in a paragraph by itself, to emphasize the situation.)

10. Now write a suitable Asking letter for the following situation:

    SITUATION: You are fresh out of college and trying to get a job as a cub reporter on a large daily newspaper, The Florida Times Union. You write Professor Lopez, your journalism professor at college, asking him to write a letter of recommendation for you to the city editor, Ralph Neeley. You also ask him to suggest another person you might ask for a reference. Since you do know the Professor, and you know that he and his family vacation at Cape Cod every summer, you may want to add a personal note about this at the very end of the letter.

> Dear Professor Lopez:
>
> I have great news! The Florida Times Union may be interested in hiring me as a cub reporter. I need some help, though.
>
> Will you be willing to write a recommendation for me to the city editor, Ralph Neeley?
>
> Also, could you suggest someone else I might ask for a reference?
>
> I hope you and your family enjoy Cape Cod this summer.

WRITING A TONGUE-IN-CHEEK ASKING LETTER

11. You can let your imagination run wild on this one. You have probably read Art Buchwald, whose column is syndicated in major newspapers throughout the United States. If so, you know that often his column is a spoof letter. His special twist is to treat a true but ridiculous event with mock seriousness.

Read this true situation. Then see if you can resolve it by writing an Art Buchwald memo to the state legislators from the Florida Attorney General, Mr. Power.

> SITUATION: There was a 40-minute power failure at Tallahassee, Florida, about a day or two after the U.S. Supreme Court put the nix on capital punishment. It so happened that the blackout interrupted a special meeting of state legislators in the basement of the State House. The purpose of this meeting was to discuss a way to pass a state law permitting capital punishment. (The electric chair hasn't been used in this country since 1967, however.) Now, Attorney General Power wants the legislators to attend another meeting to discuss the same issue--same place on Friday, at 9:00 a.m. He wants each legislator to call 774-4324 to say whether he or she will attend.

Remember, this one is just for fun! Even so, follow the general pattern for an Asking letter.

Read the suggestion. Even though it is just a silly letter (Art is still the king!), it does follow the general pattern of an Asking letter: Paragraph 1 is the Orientation; Paragraph 2 is the Information; and Paragraph 3 is the Action.

TO: Florida Legislators

FROM: Attorney General Power

The interruption of our Monday meeting was a Communist plot, obviously. But let's not give up on our goal of equal capital punishment for all just because the lights failed once. Surely we Floridians should have the power to decide what is best for our own convicts!

I suggest that we try to meet again on this matter in the basement of the State House on Friday at 9:00 a.m. And let's hope we can have all the juices flowing this time.

Please call me at 774-4324 to let me know whether we will be able to count on your spark.

OUTLINE FOR AN ASKING LETTER

12. Now, back to serious letter writing.

If you always prefer to outline before you write a long report, you would probably find it helpful to do something similar before you write a business letter. (If you are absolutely turned off by the notion of outlining, forget it was mentioned and just do the letter-writing portion of this exercise.)

For an Asking letter, you might prepare a simple form as illustrated on the following page.

ASKING LETTER

ORIENTATION:	
INFORMATION:	
ACTION:	
ADDITION:	

As you see, there is nothing magical here. You consider the same assortment of information you've been considering all along. However, the form provides a place for you to jot down your basic ideas (in sentences or not, as you like it), instead of keeping everything stored in your head. Particularly for a lengthy letter, this kind of record could be quite helpful.

Read this situation, and note how you might use it to prepare the outline for an Asking letter.

> SITUATION: You are a psychologist and belong to the American Psychological Association (APA), a national organization of psychologists. There will be an APA convention in New Orleans shortly, which you cannot attend. You notice in the brochure announcing the convention activities that one of the speakers--Dr. Jonathan Gold--will present a paper called "Foes of Learning." This sounds provocative, and you decide to write to the program chairman, Dr. Lester Paul, asking him to send you a copy of Dr. Gold's paper.

If you would like to try using the outline, write directly on the blank form on this page. Then write the letter from it. (By the way, if this system works for you, use it whenever you need to write a business letter. It is certainly handy as a checklist later, after you've written the letter, to make sure you have included all the necessary facts. If nothing else, it's a good way to get started if you have trouble facing a blank page.)

In case you don't want to use the outline, you can just write the letter below.

Compare your letter (and outline too, if you wrote one) with the suggestion(s). You may then want to do the Review of Chapter 2, on page 187, to see what you have learned. Afterwards, continue to Chapter 3, on Telling letters, and the heart of this book.

ORIENTATION:	I noted the announcement of Dr. Jonathan Gold's paper in the convention brochure.
INFORMATION:	The paper is called "Foes of Learning."
ACTION:	Please send a copy of the paper (or reprint).
ADDITION:	None

Dear Dr. Paul:

One paper listed in the APA Convention brochure interested me particularly. This was Dr. Jonathan Gold's "Foes of Learning."

Since I cannot attend the Convention this year, could you mail me a reprint? I have enclosed a self-addressed envelope and one dollar to cover the cost of postage.

CHAPTER THREE
Telling Letters

When Helen Gurley Brown became editor-in-chief of Cosmopolitan magazine, she promised many important changes--and she delivered. Articles became more thought-provoking and more sophisticated to appeal to an informed audience.

But these editorial changes might easily have gone unnoticed if Ms. Brown had not used a most unusual attention-getting device to launch the new format: a nude centerfold of Burt Reynolds, the actor.

Never mind that she had also raised the price of a single issue to one dollar. The April 1972 issue of Cosmopolitan didn't hit the newsstands: It exploded! Many newsstand dealers in downtown Manhattan sold out in half a day. Cosmopolitan was everywhere--in the newspapers, on television, on everybody's lips.

A good attention-getting device is just as important to a business letter, although it doesn't have to be so sensational. Get the reader on your side in the first paragraph--the first sentence is better--and he's likely to stay. It's a trick all good salesmen like Helen Gurley Brown know and use. And a business letter that is Telling something is really selling something too. For this reason, we construct the Telling letter from much the same viewpoint that the salesman uses to construct his sales pitch.

In this chapter you'll learn how to write letters that tell. Such letters include announcements, rejections of all sorts, apologies, adjustments, complaints, sales letters, letters written for the record, and letters to the editor. Most situations that prompt these letters are everyday things that most people know about. However, on the job and elsewhere, you may need to write Telling letters to a more specialized audience--one that uses technical terminology. The Glossary of Selected Business Terms (page 244) will help here.

Before starting the chapter, however, you may want to do the preview. The Preview to Chapter 3 is on page 189.

GENERAL PATTERN

1. The purpose of a sales pitch is to convince you to buy something that you hadn't realized you needed or perhaps even wanted. It is not just a random speech that accidentally gets you interested: It is calculated at each step to make you eager to buy.

(a) First, the salesman gets your attention and introduces you to his product. He baits the hook, either by telling you why you need this product or what will happen if you don't buy it. Or both.
(b) Next, he explains how the product works; and he demonstrates, if possible.
(c) Finally, he tries to wrap up the sale and make it easy for you to say "yes." This is known as "the close." He asks if he can sign you up, or deliver his goods to your home.

A Telling letter is organized in much the same way:

(a) First is an Orientation, in which the writer tries to get the reader's attention. Either he tells the reader why he should have the information or what will happen if he doesn't have it. Or both.
(b) Second is the Information, which contains all the relevant details. If this part is very long, it is enclosed as an attachment (or enclosure), with (at most) only a summary included in the letter proper.
(c) Next is usually the Action--some device the writer uses to determine if the reader has accepted the argument--although in some Telling letters, the Action is not stated. In many announcements, for example, readers are simply told about changes and expected to accept them. And, finally, there may be a personal Addition.

In short, a business letter should get straight to business. A Telling letter should (a) tell what you are talking about; (b) give whatever information is relevant; and (c) perhaps tell the reader what he needs to do.

Here's an illustration. Suppose Mrs. Charity Doe, a substantial contributor to the Osteomyelitis* Society, has written a letter of complaint to Director D. U. Gooder about what she feels are the Society's poor promotional techniques. Compare these two answers by Mr. Gooder. (Sample A and Sample B are on the next page.)

*A disease of the bones that attacks children.

(A)

Dear Mrs. Doe:

(a) We greatly appreciate your contribution to our great efforts to stamp out the dread disease of osteomyelitis. (b) Our efforts, as you know, are unbending. (c) We will do everything we can do to conquer this terrible crippler of small children.

(d) You have been so generous in the past that we are sorry you are unsatisfied with our work now. (e) Our program is confronted with problems. (f) Not everyone is aware of the importance of what we do.

(g) You certainly understand. (h) You are truly "Mrs. Osteomyelitis."

(B)

Dear Mrs. Doe:

(a) You have rightly complained about our promotional techniques. (b) Unfortunately, we have made mistakes. (c) However, we are learning.

(d) Although we have tried several media--TV spot ads, newspaper ads, and direct mail circulars--the return from the TV spot ads has clearly proved the best way to raise money. (e) From now on, we plan to concentrate on TV.

> (f) If you would like more details about our promotional plans, please call Miss Manage. (g) I have asked her to explain them to you.
>
> (h) Your help has been marvelous. (i) We of course hope we can continue to count on it.

You probably felt that Sample A treats Mrs. Doe as a fool by attempting to divert her complaints in an outpour of flattery. Where is the Orientation? Where is the Information? Where is Action requested? There is nothing except a muddle of empty compliments.

On the other hand, Sample B is designed to get a specific response: reestablish Mrs. Doe's confidence and thus maintain her support. It is short, simple, and sincere as well.

See if you can identify the pattern of Sample B:

(1) Which sentence(s) expresses the Orientation?______________________
(2) Which sentence(s) expresses the Information?______________________
(3) Is there an Action?_____ If so, which sentence(s) expresses it?_____
(4) Is there an Addition?_____ If so, which sentence(s) expresses it?_____

---

(1) Sentences (a), (b), and (c) express the Orientation.
(2) Sentences (d) and (e) express the Information.
(3) Yes, sentences (f) and (g).
(4) Yes, sentences (h) and (i).

KEYING THE LETTERS

2. Even though all parts of the letter are important, one part is always the key and should be emphasized. In Asking letters the key is always the Action. But in Telling letters the key varies. In a rejection, for example, the emphasis is on the Orientation because the reader first wants to know the verdict; the Information, while important, is secondary to that decision. On the other hand, the Information is the key to a letter that provides a record of facts discussed during a meeting or telephone conversation.

Read this Telling letter (it's a complaint) and note the pattern: Orientation first, Information next, and Action last.

> Dear Mr. McDonald:
>
> I have just discovered that many of the Christie Club luncheons were charged to my personal account rather than to the Christie Club account.
>
> Enclosed is a list of all the items that are currently charged to my account, No. 7778. The circled items should instead be charged to No. 7779, which is the Christie account number.
>
> Please send me a revised listing of the charges to both the Christie account and to my own account.

Which part of this letter do you think is the key? Explain why.

The Orientation is probably the key. Once the reader knows what the complaint is all about, he probably knows the Action he is expected to take. The only part that may be missing is the list of details in the Information.

UNUSUAL LETTER

3. In the rest of this chapter, you're going to consider each kind of conventional Telling letter: sales, announcement, rejection, letter for the record, adjustment and complaint, and letter to the editor. You will trace the pattern and construct letters in response to given situations. As you will see, having a pattern to follow greatly simplifies the letter writing.

But maybe you're thinking that patterns are rules, and that rules destroy creativity. Not at all. In fact, the variations on the pattern can be infinite. A good case in point is Sample A, an actual letter written by a young lawyer to an opponent who lost his nerve in a suit.

(A)

Dear Fred,

There once was a plaintiff named
Fred,
Whose suit was brought
"Full steam ahead";
But when defendant said
"settle,"
And tested Fred's
mettle,
Not a word by ol' Fred
was e'er said.

Sincerely,

Ira Krakower

Unorthodox, yes. Yet maybe this was the only effective way to chide Fred without angering him. More important for our purpose here, the letter consists of an Orientation supported by Information. So, the unconventional limerick really follows the conventional pattern.

Ira Krakower's complaint letter is not an isolated sample. Sample B, a sarcastic announcement from Anonymous, illustrates another unusual variation.

(B)

TO: All Employees

FROM: Anonymous

(a) Effective immediately
a new tax will be withheld
from your pay check.

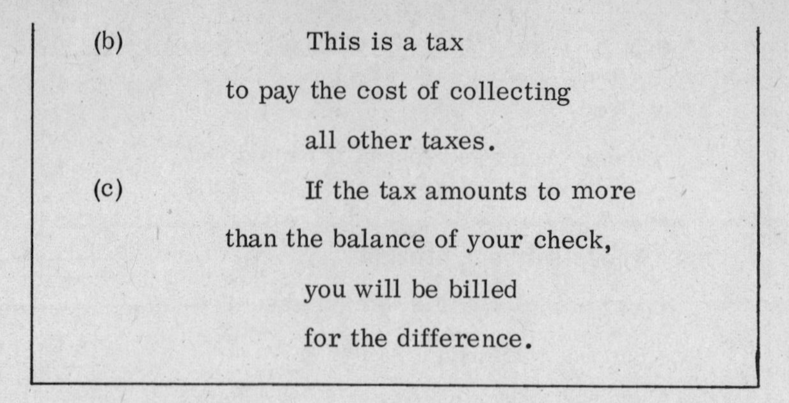
(b) This is a tax
to pay the cost of collecting
all other taxes.
(c) If the tax amounts to more
than the balance of your check,
you will be billed
for the difference.

Even though it is unconventional, Sample B follows the pattern.
(1) Which sentence(s) expresses the Orientation?____________________
(2) Which sentence(s) expresses the Information?____________________
(3) Which sentence(s) expresses the Action?____________________

---

(1) Sentence (a) expresses the Orientation.
(2) Sentences (b) and (c) express the Information.
(3) None (The action is understood.)

SALES LETTER

4. Let's get back to more conventional letters. First, we will look at the sales (or promotion) letter. As you learned earlier, a good sales pitch follows the pattern of a business letter. And a good sales letter must be more than a sales pitch because it must be more persuasive, relying on the written word only and not on demonstrations and sparkling personality.

The sales letter has an Orientation to interest the reader in a product or a service; it has relevant Information; and it has an Action--some device that will urge the reader to a decision about buying.

An Addition--some personal comment--could really be a plus providing it comes at the beginning of the letter. An addition at the end of the letter could interfere with the Action--the close of the sale. And always keep in mind that anything interfering with the close could also spoil the sale.

We get so many sales pressures from all sources that a sales pitch has to be good. If not, we tune it out unheard or toss it away unread. This means that we must be sure to emphasize the right part of the sales letter.

But which part is the key? This depends on what you're trying to sell. If your product or service is new and sensational, you should emphasize the Orientation. If your product or service is a common one that has many competitors but is superior to them, you should emphasize the Information. On the other hand, if your product or service has many competitors but is not demonstrably superior, you had better emphasize the Action. And you can take a tip here from the sellers of soaps and breakfast cereals. With nothing special to offer in the product, they bribe the buyers with unrelated giveaways or coupons--anything to draw the buyers to their products rather than to those of their competitors.

To summarize:

(a) For something new, emphasize the Orientation.
(b) For something competitive but superior, emphasize the Information.
(c) For something with many equal competitors, emphasize the Action--that is, make it easy for the reader to take.

Read this selling letter, and note the pattern and the emphasis.

Dear Friend,

Here's a sample copy of the Westsider, a weekly newspaper which will be covering the West Side of Manhattan from 59th Street to 125th Street.

Some of the things we'll be covering will be housing, drugs, crime, health problems, education and stories about people and organizations in your community. There will also be a calendar of events listing what's happening on the West Side each week. We'll have columns and reviews too.

We're just beginning, and we need your support. Our charter subscription rates are extremely low: $2.00 for one year, $3.50 for two, and $5.00 for three.

> So . . . mail in your check in the attached envelope and give us a try. You won't be sorry!
>
> Cordially,
>
> Joan Buckley
>
> Joan Buckley
> Circulation Department

What seems to be the key here?________________________________

_ _ _ _ _ _ _ _ _ _ _ _ _ _ _

The Information.

5. Remember that having a pattern doesn't mean that you have to write rigid business letters, with each part in a separate paragraph. You won't do this if you consider the letter parts as functions, rather than mechanical structures.

Here is a dandy letter that tries to sell you a membership in a record club. As you read it, try to identify its pattern and decide what is emphasized.

> Dear Friend:
>
> (a) As Executive Director of Columbia House, I can't imagine a better offer than 12 best-selling albums for only $1.00. But then, you might be thinking we have something else up our sleeve; that the offer is too good to be true; that there's a "catch."
>
> (b) WELL, THERE IS. THIS INCREDIBLE SAVINGS IS AVAILABLE ONLY TO PEOPLE WHO BUY AT LEAST FIVE MORE RECORDS A YEAR FROM THE CLUB.

(c) With at least five sales from each of the more than two million members of Columbia House, we know that our volume will be greater by far than any store, anywhere. Of course, we can sell records for less than anyone else does!

(d) To put it another way, thanks to the Club plan, YOU CAN'T BUY RECORDS REGULARLY FOR LESS ANYWHERE. Never. Because after you complete your original agreement, WE GIVE YOU ONE RECORD FREE FOR EVERY ONE YOU BUY.

(e) So there it is. Not a "catch," but a real chance for record buyers to enjoy the top stars from more than 50 different recording companies at the best possible price.

(f) If there's anything I haven't covered, anything that still bothers you, please do take the moment I asked for to tell me what it is. (Use the enclosed postpaid reply envelope.) I would greatly appreciate it.

Yours truly,
David Stewart
David Stewart
Executive Director
Columbia House

(1) Which part is the key?______________ Explain why.______________

____

____

(2) Which paragraph(s) expresses the Orientation?____________________
(3) Which paragraph(s) expresses the Information?____________________
(4) Which paragraph(s) expresses the Action?________________________

- - - - - - - - - - - - - - -

(1) The key is probably the Information, because it explains why the offer is superior.
(2) Paragraph (a) expresses the Orientation.
(3) Paragraphs (b), (c), (d), and (e) express the Information.
(4) Paragraph (f) expresses the Action.

6. Read the two letters in this exercise and then decide which part you think is the key of each.

(A)

> Dear Friend:
>
> Do you get only one television channel on your set? And is your reception on that channel poor?
>
> If your answer to both questions is "yes," you need Largo Cable Television Service!* For as little as $5 a month, you can have your pick of four different channels--and excellent reception on each.
>
> Please mail the enclosed postcard today, and our representative will call you for an appointment.
>
> Largo Cable Television Service

Key to Sample A:____

____

*Cable television is a special system with underground cables, so that interference is minimized.

____

(B)

> Dear Neighbor:
>
> Please accept this half-price ticket to the Riviera Theater, 44 Main Street, as our gift. You may use it any weekday.
>
> We hope to see you weekends too, since we always have a good show at the Riviera.
>
> Management, Riviera Theater

Key to Sample B: ____

____

Sample A: The key is the Orientation. (Cable television service offers a unique product that the reader will buy if he is persuaded that he needs it.)
Sample B: The key is the Action. (The whole letter consists of Action.)

7. Ordinarily, a postscript (P.S.) is not used in a business letter, since the P.S. is reserved for an afterthought. And you ordinarily want to give the impression that anything related to the business at hand is a main thought. But in the sales letter the postscript may be exactly right as a way to express part or all of the Action. You then seem to be using only low-pressure sales techniques.

Use this postscript technique and the following facts to write a sales letter:

(a) You are Graham Krahker, and you own a cottage in the Berkshire Mountains that you want to rent for the summer. You have an interested prospective tenant, Mr. Acropolis.
(b) The house has four bedrooms, a stone fireplace in the living room, and all modern appliances in the kitchen. It is completely furnished, even to books and games.
(c) There are twenty wooded acres and a brook stocked with fish.
(d) There is good boating and swimming too in nearby lakes.
(e) The rent is $2,000 for ten weeks.
(f) Mr. Acropolis may call collect at (212) 834-8990. (Hint: Make this a postscript.)

____

____

Dear Mr. Acropolis:

You would love my house. [Orientation]

It has four bedrooms, a stone fireplace in the living room, and all modern appliances in the kitchen. Of course, it is completely furnished--even with books and games. [Information]

The property itself is beautiful too. There are twenty wooded acres and a brook stocked with fish. If you want water sports, there are several lakes nearby. [Information]

Everything can be yours for ten weeks and for only $2,000. Do we have a deal? [Information, Action]

Sincerely yours,
Graham Krahker
Graham Krahker

P.S. You may call me collect at (212) 834-8990.

ANNOUNCEMENT

8. Next, let's look at the simple announcement of some decision or event.

As you'll see, an announcement follows the general pattern of Orientation and Information--but only sometimes an Action, since this is usually understood. However, the Orientation is the key, with the Information secondary.

The Orientation explains the news event and what it will mean to the reader--perhaps what would happen if he did not read it. The Information gives the details, but in a separate paragraph or paragraphs. If there is an Action--something the writer wants the reader to do to prove that he accepts the verdict--it is usually set off by itself.

Overall, a simple announcement, like every other business letter, should be short, simple, and sincere. It should also be timely, following shortly after the event.

Read this simple announcement that circulated around Manhattan offices after the Burt Reynolds centerfold appeared. Note how the letter, though meant to be humorous, still follows the general pattern.

Dear ________________:

(a) Your body has been submitted as a possible candidate for our COSMOPOLITAN Centerfold. As you know, this is a unique opportunity for notoriety.

(b) Our foldouts represent not only the epitomy of true masculinity, but of intellect as well. Our judges are all impartial: Selections are made on the basis of merit, subscribers' recommendations, or whatever.

(c) If you accept this honor and wish to be considered further, promptly return the enclosed form and an 8 x 10 glossy.

Helen Envy Green
COSMOPOLITAN Representative
(Foldout Recruiting Department)

Note particularly how the writer made certain he would know how the reader responded.

Describe briefly what each paragraph does.

Paragraph (a):______________________________

Paragraph (b):______________________________

Paragraph (c):______________________________

Paragraph (a) announces the event (Orientation).
Paragraph (b) explains the honor (Information).
Paragraph (c) specifies what the reader must do (Action).

9. The most common reason a Telling letter fails is that it mires the reader in details before orienting him to the situation. If you arouse his interest first, he is likely to stay with you through the details. And if you want him to respond, you should close by suggesting a simple way to do it.

Read this simple announcement. As you'll see, it fails because it plunges the reader into details before telling him what the message is all about.

MEMO TO ALL EMPLOYEES

_____ Our major cost here is people. _____ By this I mean people's time, which the company must reimburse with money. _____ Our other expenditures, it may surprise you to learn, are small by comparison. _____ I'm not trying to check up on you--that's a promise. _____ I'm trying to figure out the cost of producing our materials. _____ Will you help me by completing a DAILY COST ACCOUNTING form? _____ Please give your form to the receptionist each day as you leave the office. _____ And, by the way, the form may need some changes. _____ If you can think of ways to simplify it, please tell me.

Did you have to reread the memo? That would be ironic here, since the writer claims that the major cost in his office is people's time. Is all of it spent in reading memos like this?

Yet the memo could be extremely effective with just some simple rearrangements. Number the sentences in the memo in what you would think is an effective sequence. Also insert the paragraphing symbol where you think a new paragraph should begin.

The sentences might be numbered in this order:
4, 5, 6, 2, 3, 1, 7, 8, and 9.

The revised letter would then be paragraphed as follows:

> Will you help me by completing a DAILY COST ACCOUNTING form? I'm not trying to check up on you--that's a promise. I'm trying to figure out the cost of producing our materials.
>
> Our major cost here is people. By this I mean people's time, which the company must reimburse with money. Our other expenditures, it may surprise you to learn, are small by comparison.
>
> Please give your form to the receptionist each day as you leave the office. And, by the way, the form may need some changes. If you can think of ways to simplify it, please tell me.

10. Pace College, a Manhattan school specializing in business courses, tried an unusual experiment in the summer of 1972. They called it "Lunch & Learn." (They probably should have called it "Luncheon Learn," or "Lunch 'N Learn.") Read the following situation which describes it, and then try to write an announcement addressed to the students of Pace. (Hint: The Action can be an invitation to the first lecture.)

SITUATION: The Lunch & Learn program is an opportunity to combine a pleasant lunch with a pleasant setting and some intellectual stimulation. Each Tuesday and Thursday during July and August, a Pace faculty member will address the luncheon group on a topic of interest related to his expertise. The first talk will be this Tuesday, by Dr. Joseph E. Houle, Dean of the School of Arts and Sciences. His topic is "The Humane Businessman: The Liberal Arts in Management." The cost for the buffet luncheon is $2.14; the place is the Faculty Dining Room; and the time is 12:00 noon.

---- ---- ------

TO: All Students

We're trying something new in this Summer of '72: what we call "Lunch & Learn." [Orientation]

Every Tuesday and Wednesday at noon during July and August, we'll gather in the Faculty Dining Room at 12:00 noon for a buffet lunch and a talk by one of our faculty members--something light to go with the lunch and yet informative. The cost is just $2.14 a person. [Information]

Please join us this Tuesday to hear Dr. Joseph E. Houle, Dean of the School of Arts and Sciences. Dr. Houle will speak on the topic "The Humane Businessman: The Liberal Arts in Management." [Action, Information]

REJECTION

11. Not all announcements are good or interesting or even controversial. Some tell unhappy news, such as the rejection of a piece of writing or a job. Since such news will fall on unwilling ears, the writer of the letter should concentrate on getting the right tone.

Again, the Orientation is the key. In fact, not much more is required. Information is not necessary. But if it is volunteered, it must sound sincere. The reader learns he has been rejected. He would like to know why, but he doesn't really care as much about the details as he does about the fact of rejection.

Since a rejection is the end of the line, usually there is no Action. On the other hand, a sincere Addition will make the reader feel better. As you recall, an Addition in an Asking letter is personal and of course reserved for someone you know. But a simple, impersonal Addition like "Good luck in getting a job" is appropriate in a rejection whether you know the person or not.

One word of warning, however. Please don't tell the rejected applicant that you'll keep his letter on file and call him if you need someone. This line is insincere. Why would a good applicant still be around when you're ready to hire the next time? And if you would hire him the next time, why not this time? Shopping around for a new employee is like shopping for a house. You can buy only what is available. Somebody buys the good house. Somebody hires the good potential employee. Each time you look for a new house or someone to hire, you have a different set to pick from. The rejected applicant knows this too.

Another point to remember is that being nice doesn't make a rejection easier to accept. But you can be straightforward without being blunt. The important point is to get the business done--and also be nice.

Try to identify the pattern of the following rejection.

Dear Ms. Cohen:

I am sorry that I don't have better news for you. As you know, there were many qualified applicants. However, I have decided to hire a young man who has had a great deal of experience working in biological laboratories.

Your qualifications are good, and I know you will find something suitable very soon.

Sincerely,
Lottie Luck
Lottie Luck

Did you notice that the writer never actually said she was rejecting the applicant? It wasn't necessary. By combining the Orientation and the Information in the first paragraph, she was able to convey the message without stating the dreaded words. (This is not always possible, however.)

(a) Why was the applicant rejected? ______________________________

____

____

(b) What device did the writer use to close? ______________________

____

- - - - - - - - - - - - - - -

(a) Another applicant was better qualified.
(b) She ended on a positive note (by expressing confidence that Ms. Cohen would soon get a job).

12. Not all rejections are written to job applicants. Sometimes suggestions are rejected; at times, requests have to be denied. All rejections follow the same general pattern, however.

Keep in mind that the Orientation is the key to a rejection that lets the person down as gently as possible. But this doesn't mean that the writer should give all the details before giving the verdict.

Read the following rejection, and decide how it could be improved. Assume it is from a fan club of the New York Mets baseball players.

> Dear Met Fan:
>
> (a) Every year, many fans ask if we can supply pictures of their favorite Met baseball players. (b) I wish we could supply photographs of the players. (c) But photographs are expensive. (d) Unfortunately, we can't afford to send them--even to interested fans like you.
>
> (e) But please continue rooting for the Mets. (f) And come out to see the Mets at Shea Stadium.

To make this an effective letter, some cutting would be healthy here.
(1) Which sentence(s) would you cut? _______
(2) Explain briefly why the cutting would improve the letter. _________

____

- - - - - - - - - - - - - -

(1) Sentences (a) and (c) could be dropped.
(2) These sentences contain only unnecessary details.

13. Some of the private schools in Manhattan are courted by so many parents that babies must be registered at birth, it seems, to be assured of entering the "right" kindergartens. This is true even in recession years, when money is tight.

Assume you are the director of such a school, called High Grammar School. Using a separate sheet of paper, write a letter of rejection to the parents of preschooler Roy Brown in response to the following situation:

> SITUATION: All the kindergarten places for the fall term of High Grammar School were filled well before Mr. and Mrs. Brown applied--even though they had applied a full year before Roy was eligible for admission. You must reject the application, but you want the tone of this letter to be extremely friendly. You also want to suggest that the Browns apply elsewhere, since many good schools are still accepting applications.

> Dear Mr. and Mrs. Brown:
>
> I am sorry to tell you that we can't admit Roy to High Grammar School next year, since our places for kindergarten have already been filled. [Orientation, Information]
>
> Many fine schools are still accepting kindergarten applications, however. I feel certain that you will find a suitable place for Roy. [Addition]

LETTER FOR THE RECORD

14. A verbal agreement is often called a gentleman's agreement. Yet business people have learned that a gentleman's agreement is always more gentlemanly (and more of an agreement) when it is in writing.

Most business people make a habit of writing down the results of a meeting or telephone conversation. They do so because human beings tend to remember what they would like to have happened rather than what actually took place. The recording of these events is called a "letter for the record" because it stands as evidence of what really happened. It is always a reference afterwards, if any misunderstandings arise between the parties involved.

The letter for the record follows the general pattern for Telling letters. But the key is always the Information. Obviously, each detail must be stated, and it must be stated accurately. Usually there is an Action, which asks the reader whether he agrees to the Information. And there may be an Addition.

Assume you are the publisher, Apple & Sons. Write a satisfactory letter for the record, on a separate sheet of paper, using the following facts:

(a) There was a meeting yesterday between an author, Guy Wyer, and his publisher, Apple & Sons.
(b) The author agreed to produce a 250-page book on popular song writers. The first draft is due in six months.
(c) The publisher will furnish a $5,000 advance immediately on 15-percent royalties--also, typing help.
(d) The publisher will mail the contracts for the author's signature within a week.

Dear Mr. Wyer:

We covered so much ground at our meeting yesterday that I thought I should summarize our agreements. [Orientation]

We are delighted that you will write a 250-page book for Apple & Sons on popular song writers. The first draft will be due in six months. For our part, we will give you a $5,000 advance immediately on the 15-percent royalties. We will also give you any typing help you might need. [Information]

If I don't hear from you within a week, I will assume that our agreement is satisfactory, and will mail you the contracts. [Action]

COMPLAINT AND ADJUSTMENT

15. Comedian Don Rickles once said to his TV boss, "I see by the expression on your face that you haven't read my letter of resignation, which I wrote in the heat of my stupidity."

That says it for the angry letter. Never, never write one. But if you are tempted, write your angry letter and put it aside, at least overnight. Read it the next morning, when you're not in the "heat of your stupidity," and assess it. If you have a single doubt about sending it, the very firm rule is: DON'T DO IT!

This doesn't mean you should never write a letter of complaint. But send it to someone who can take the necessary Action. You can serve no purpose by telling the caretaker that computers are not being introduced properly or by telling the sales clerk that the credit system is mismanaged. Such complaints should be made to the managers themselves. If you don't know who the managers are, make your points directly to the presidents of the companies.

Something else to consider before you send a complaint is that you had better be able to support everything you say. Otherwise, you may be damaging another person's reputation. There are libel laws to protect people from character assassination, and you could be hit with an expensive, ugly law suit if you say ugly things that aren't true.

Assuming the complaint is legitimate, the key to the letter is probably the Orientation. However, the Information here is nearly as important. Not only must the details be accurate, but they must also be relevant.

Read this complaint about a defective electric yogurt maker, and consider how the letter could be improved.

> Dear Mr. Sawyer:
>
> (a) The yogurt maker that I bought from Macy's arrived Friday, February 18, 1973.
>
> (b) But so far I have been unable to make yogurt.
>
> (c) Last night's experiment was my eighth try.
>
> (d) I still get curdled milk whenever I try to make yogurt with my Yogurtera.

(e) I have tried letting the boiled milk cool for less than 30 minutes, since I thought perhaps it had been too cool to grow bacteria.

(f) But now I have run out of experiments.

(g) Can you help me?

Sincerely

May Bee Dumm

May Bee Dumm

This low-key complaint is refreshing: It carries no dire threats, and it doesn't sound as if life will stop just because the yogurt maker isn't making yogurt. Remember that threats and anger are unnecessary with reputable business people, and they are ineffective with the unscrupulous ones. (You need a lawyer for such people.) Good business people want satisfied customers, and they will respond to a reasonable complaint.

Nevertheless, May Bee Dumm's complaint was diluted by unnecessary details. The letter would have been more effective with some careful cutting. Which sentence(s) would you cut?

------ ---- ----

Sentences (a), (b), and (c) could have been cut.
Sentence (a) contains unnecessary details: Where Ms. Dumm bought the Yogurtera and when it arrived are not relevant. Sentence (d) carries the information given in sentences (b) and (c).

16. A complaint needs an answer. And the answer--the adjustment--also follows the same pattern of Orientation, Information, and Action. But the key to the adjustment letter is usually the Action.

Decide whether this answer to May Bee Dumm about her nonfunctional Yogurtera is a satisfactory reply.

Dear Ms. Dumm:

Sorry you are having no luck at all in making yogurt.

There are just two ways to go wrong:

a) You can move the milk mixture before the six-hour fermentation period has ended; or

b) You can cover the brewing jar with the WHITE storage cap instead of the RED cap during the fermentation period.

If you haven't done either of these, your unit is probably defective. Please return it to us, and we will replace it for you.

Sincerely yours,

Nick Sawyer

Nick Sawyer

You probably agree that this is a satisfactory letter. Note that the strategy was first to express sympathy, next explain what might have gone wrong, and then offer to replace the unit. How would you explain this strategy as part of a Telling letter? ____________________

____

- - - - - - - - - - - - - -

The sympathetic approach is the Orientation; the explanation of what might have gone wrong is the Information; and the replacement offer is the Action.

17. Many department stores now use computers in their billing departments. This means that unless customers pay their bills within a few days (usually ten), they automatically get a reminder to pay. This practice is often annoying to the conscientious customer who for some good reason is occasionally slow in paying the bill.

Assume you are Mrs. Minnie Dymunds, a customer who travels a great deal and also makes large purchases at Toney's Department

Store in Chicago. You have just returned to town and have discovered a form letter from Toney's reminding you to pay. You are annoyed. Write a letter of complaint to the credit department at Toney's. Be nice but firm. (Address your letter to "Gentlemen.")

----- ----------

Gentlemen:

Among my many letters, magazines, and second-class mail was a reminder from Toney's that my bill was overdue. This has happened before, when I have been unavoidably late in paying, but by just a few days. [Orientation, Information]

I suppose your policy is to send out such reminders whether a customer is normally prompt to pay or not. I also suppose the computers are partly to blame. Nevertheless, I hope you will consider making an exception

for good customers and allowing a month to pass
before sending a reminder about an unpaid
balance. [Information, Action]

Sincerely yours,
Minnie Dymunds
Minnie Dymunds

18. Mr. Buck Passer, manager of the Credit Department of Toney's Department Store, knows he must answer Mrs. Dymunds' reasonable complaint. Unfortunately, he can't do anything about the situation other than tell Mrs. Dymunds to ignore these reminders. They are unavoidable now because of the way the computers are programmed. However, the manager can tell Mrs. Dymunds that he will present the problem to Mr. Toney himself and suggest that the computers be programmed to delay a month before such form reminders are sent out.

Write this letter to Mrs. Dymunds.

--- -- ---- -- ----

Dear Mrs. Dymunds:

As you have correctly surmised, the computers are to blame for all those nagging payment reminders. I am truly sorry they have been such a nuisance. [Orientation, Information]

Unfortunately, we cannot promise to remedy this situation soon. However, your letter did stimulate me to discuss the matter with Mr. Toney. Perhaps we can arrange things so reminders will be delayed for a month. I will let you know. Meanwhile, please excuse us and ignore any more of those form reminders. [Information, Action]

Sincerely yours,

Buck Passer

Buck Passer

LETTER TO THE EDITOR

19. We shall finally look at the letter to the editor, which is not strictly a business letter. It is included here because it can be a lesson in good letter-writing patterns as well as in the strategy of being short, simple, and sincere.

Although people write to the editor for many reasons, the most compelling motivation is to persuade the reader to a particular opinion. The key, then, is usually the Information. However, this kind of Telling letter introduces another dimension as well: the level of the audience. To be effective, the letter to the editor should reach the level it aims at.

As a case in point, let's consider an actual letter to the editor written by a resident of Glen Cove, Long Island. The letter was written after the writer's neighbors failed to support a referendum that would have pumped money into the Glen Cove school system. For some strange reason, the letter was popular among those on both sides of the issue. Decide whether you think Mr. Sage was disappointed or pleased that the referendum didn't pass.

To the Editor: Close the Schools?

The people of Glen Cove have spoken. The School Board's mandate is clear. The resounding defeat of the school tax referendum is not merely a vote for less education--it is an overwhelming vote for no education at all voiced loud and clear by those who did not vote at all. If the School Board has a decent respect for the will of the community, it has no choice but to close the schools at once.

This is a breathtaking idea, one that could only have come from the people in their wisdom. Not only will school taxes not rise--they will disappear entirely. Moreover, the proceeds realized from the sale of various school properties will pay for civic improvements that are really necessary.

The high school alone will bring in enough to build an olympic-sized saltwater pool at Prybil Beach, with enough left over to make the back nine at the golf course a lot more interesting. Our boatmen can look forward to a spruced-up marina.

What about the kids? Well, what about them? What law says we have to have kids in Glen Cove? Let people with kids move them to Great Neck or Plainview or some other place where people believe in spending money on education.

David Sage
4 Viola Drive

Did you decide that Mr. Sage was for the referendum and was deeply disappointed that it didn't pass? If so, you were right. It's a great letter. Unfortunately, most of the Glen Cove residents didn't understand it: They all decided that David Sage was on their side. He failed to score his point, even though he wrote beautifully.

People tend to read what they want to hear. There is a lesson here, though: Persuading someone to your point of view is not a simple task. The direct approach is still better. Had David made a direct appeal to those who disagreed with him, he might have made a few of them guilty.

Sample B illustrates this direct approach in the Information portion of a letter to the editor. James Reston of The New York Times wrote this letter a few days after Harry Truman unexpectedly defeated Thomas E. Dewey for the presidency in 1948. In analyzing the situation, Mr. Reston made the following statements about the press:

(B)

"In a way our failure was not unlike Mr. Dewey's; we overestimated the tangibles and underestimated intangibles; we relied too much on techniques of reporting which are no longer foolproof; just as he was too isolated with other politicians, so were we too isolated with other reporters, and we, too, were far too impressed by the tidy statistics of the polls."

> "The great intangible of this election was the political thinking of the Roosevelt era on the nation . . . and we did not give enough weight to it. Consequently we were wrong, not only about the election, but, what's worse, on the whole political direction of our time."

Can you guess what Mr. Reston's Orientation was?____________________

____

Both the press and the pollsters failed to assess the political scene accurately. (The direct approach here left no doubt as to Mr. Reston's argument.)

20. Vermont is a rare state that does not permit roadside billboards. Assume you are a citizen of another state where billboards are permitted. Write a letter to the editor of a prominent newspaper of your state suggesting that billboards be banned.

Letter to the Editor:

Out for a drive in the country: BUY GETTY GAS, DRINK COCA COLA, EAT WONDER BREAD, VISIT LURAY CAVERNS, STOP AT BASKETVILLE, NEXT STOP STUCKEY'S PECANS . . . . We are assaulted mile after mile. Where are the trees? [Information, Orientation]

We're told that billboard advertising is necessary to business and that it should be encouraged. Besides, it brings in added revenue to highway property owners. [Information]

But what about the countryside we can no longer see? Soon there will be too little of it left to see. [Information]

Let's join Vermont and ban billboards. [Action]

CHART AND OUTLINE

21. In a sense, a Telling letter is the key to Communicating By Letter: If you can write a Telling letter, you know most of what you need to know about writing business communications.

The chart on the next page will help you recall the important features of the Telling letter. It will also help you prepare an outline (assuming that you find outlines useful). Look over this chart now.

TYPE	KEY		OUTLINE
(1) Sales letter (a) For unusual product (b) For competitive but superior product (c) For competitive but ordinary product	(a) Orientation (b) Information (c) Action	(1)	Addition:
			Orientation
			Information:
			Action:
(2) Announcement	Orientation	(2)	Orientation:
			Information:
			Action:
(3) Rejection	Orientation	(3)	Orientation:
			Information:
			Action:
			Addition:
(4) Letter for the record	Information	(4)	Orientation:
			Information:
			Action:
			Addition:
(5) Complaint and Adjustment (a) Complaint (b) Adjustment	(a) Orientation (b) Action	(5)	Orientation:
			Information:
			Action:
			Addition:
(6) Letter to the editor	Information	(6)	Orientation:
			Information:
			Action:
			Addition:

As you see, the chart is not only useful, but it is also easy to use. Just decide the kind of letter you need to write; note the key; and outline the relevant facts. Try it now, from the following situation. Then write a letter. Of course, if you are absolutely opposed to using outlines for writing, you may skip the outline here and write the letter directly.

> SITUATION: You are Paul Lett, director of a summer day camp called Mount Paul. In April you decide to write the parents of last year's campers to describe the program for the coming season and to interest them in sending their kids this year. In addition to last year's sports and arts and crafts programs, there is guitar instruction by Mr. Blooz Singer, a high school music teacher with ten years' experience. There will also be two-wheeler bike instruction twice a week and pony riding once a week. These two activities are new. You suggest that interested parents fill out the application and reserve places for their children now, since you are expecting a record turnout.

Compare your outline and letter with the following suggestions. Then you may want to do the Review of Chapter 3 (page 191) before you consider Chapter 4 and letters that Build Good Will.

TYPE	KEY	OUTLINE
(1) Sales letter		(1) Addition: Hope they have had a productive year.
(a) For unusual product	(a) Orientation	Orientation: A brand-new camp season is coming up, with the best offering ever.
(b) For competitive but superior product	(b) Information	Information: Besides last year's sports and arts and crafts, Blooz Singer, high school music teacher with ten years' experience, will teach guitar; two-wheeler bike instruction twice a week; pony riding once a week.
(c) For competitive but ordinary product	(c) Action	Action: Send in application in enclosed envelope to be sure of a place.

Dear Parents:

I hope you have had a most productive year, and now are making summer fun plans for your children that include Camp Paul. You will be happy to know that we are expecting a record enrollment for the coming day camp season, in what promises to be our best and most varied program ever. [Addition, Orientation]

In addition to our usual sports and arts and crafts, we will be offering guitar lessons from Mr. Blooz Singer, an accomplished guitarist with ten years' experience as a high school music teacher. [Information]

We will also have two-wheeler bike instruction twice a week and pony riding once a week. [Information]

Won't you please complete the application form, and use the enclosed envelope to mail it to me right away so I can reserve a place for your youngster this summer? [Action]

Sincerely yours,

Paul Lett

Paul Lett

CHAPTER FOUR

Building Good Will

This is the letter that businessmen don't have to write, but do, because it can work--it really can build good will. Here is an example of a situation that inspires--and gets--good will because of a successful Building Good Will letter.

Friday morning, Fred Cook and his wife brought their first baby home from the hospital. Over the weekend, everyone in the Cook household forgot what sleep was, but Monday morning meant business as usual in the office. Fortunately, Fred found the following letter on his desk:

> Dear Fred,
>
> Or should I say "Dear Dad"?
>
> Congratulations to you and your wife! I know you're both very happy.
>
> Cordially,
>
> Jim
>
> Jim Bastion

Well, wasn't that friendly of old Jim? How did he find out? Jim Bastion makes it his business to find out such things. He combs the local newspapers for new items about his customers and he uses any slim excuse to write. The strategy is to make sure his customers always have a pleasant image of him. Obviously, he wants customers to buy from him instead of from his competitors.

This chapter covers letters whose short-term objective is to give their readers unexpected pleasure. In the long run, these letters will also Build Good Will. These are the letters included in the category of "miscellaneous": expressions of thanks, regret, sympathy, appreciation--all the letters you don't actually have to write, but which pay dividends if you do.

Traditional salespeople are not the only ones who should learn how to write a Building Good Will letter. In a sense, we are all selling something, whether it is know-how, services, actual products, or maybe even a reputation as a nice guy.

Before you start the chapter, however, you might do the Preview to Chapter 4 on page 193 to see which exercises you should concentrate on.

PATTERN OF A BUILDING GOOD WILL LETTER

1. As you know, all Asking and most Telling letters conclude by suggesting some Action for the reader to take. But the Building Good Will letter is an exception to the usual kind of business letter because it doesn't expect the reader to do anything. As a result, it follows a slightly different pattern.

First, some Occasion inspires the letter. This may be something pleasant, like a birth, a wedding, a promotion, or an anniversary. Or it may be something unfortunate, like an error or even a death. In turn, this occasion inspires the Expression, which is actually the heart of the Good Will letter. In fact, sometimes that's all there is. Action is never a part of this kind of letter, although sometimes there is a personal Addition.

But, like every other kind of business letter, the Building Good Will letter should be short, simple, and sincere. And to be most effective, it must also be timely, of course. As you read the sample letter that follows, see if you can identify the pattern.

> Dear Claire,
>
> (1) Paul Beldon sent me a copy of your guest editorial, "Why Not Fire the Teachers?" (2) It's great! (3) I think you and I agree that middle-class parents often meddle so much that they muddle the teachers.

(4) We haven't talked for ages. (5) I hope we'll get the chance at the teachers' convention in Atlantic City.

Sincerely,
Mary
Mary Donley

Now answer these questions. (Give the number, or numbers, of the sentences.)
(a) What part of the letter is the Occasion?________________
(b) What part is the Expression?________________
(c) What part is the Addition?________________

(a) Sentence (1) states the Occasion.
(b) Sentence (2) is the Expression. You might have said sentence (3) as well.
(c) Sentences (4) and (5) make up the Addition.

2. Most people expect consistently good service from the business people they deal with. But sometimes there are special, understandable reasons for a lapse in the usual service. Such instances should be explained if a company expects to maintain the good will of its customers.

Here is a special Building Good Will letter that the Doubleday Book Club sent to its customers to apologize for an unavoidable delay in service.

Dear Member:

(a) The recent floods caused by Hurricane Agnes devastated widespread areas of the eastern section of the country. ________________

(b) Our warehouse and shipping facilities and the service post office in Pennsylvania are located in areas that were directly in the path of the storm, and unfortunately they suffered considerable damage.________________ (c) We are making every effort to restore our facilities; but if you should notice a delay in our service, we hope you'll be patient and understand that we are doing our best to resume normal operations. ________________

(d) Thank you for your patience and cooperation. ________________

Membership Secretary

There is no way to know how many people would have complained or--worse--how many would have canceled their memberships. Doubleday wisely didn't wait to find out. Instead, it seized the opportunity to Build Good Will.

Recalling the parts of the Building Good Will letter, label each sentence in the sample Doubleday letter.

- - - - - - - - - - - - - - -

(a) Occasion
(b) Information or a continuation of the Occasion
(c) Expression
(d) Expression

MENTIONING THE OCCASION

3. Even though the Occasion is the spur to the Building Good Will letter, it doesn't necessarily have to be a part of it. If the Occasion is obvious, why mention it? The Expression is enough. But if the reader needs some orientation, the Occasion becomes an essential.

As an example, suppose citizen Tom O'Toole had sent sample A to the President of the United States shortly after he had won the 1976 election. What would you think of his letter?

(A)

> Dear Mr. President:
>
> Congratulations on being elected President of the United States!
>
> Cordially,
> Thomas O'Toole
> Thomas O'Toole

As if the President didn't know why congratulations were in order! It is ridiculous.

Sample Letter B, another example, was written by a secretary who forgot to enclose a promised pamphlet with a previous letter to Mr. Russo. In answer to his inquiry, she sent the pamphlet with just this brief covering apology:

(B)

> Dear Mr. Russo:
>
> Sorry.
>
> Sincerely,
> Michelle Gitlin
> Michelle Gitlin

Ms. Gitlin's letter was short, simple, and sincere. She had made only a small error, and the pamphlet was sufficient orientation--particularly since Mr. Russo had written to ask for it.

A person who is very busy or who gets lots of mail needs some orientation, however. The Occasion that inspires the Building Good Will letter sometimes needs to be mentioned. Sample B (above) would not have been sufficient for the president of Motorola or Western Electric. The decision to include or omit the Occasion rests upon the particular reader's need for an orientation.

Suppose an employer has sent you a check for some freelance typing you did for him. You want to thank him, but briefly. Do you think reply (a) or reply (b) is better? Explain why.

(a) Thanks so much.
(b) Thanks so much for the check.

Reply (b) is better. Mentioning the check orients the busy employer to the letter immediately. He doesn't have to search his memory to find out why he is being thanked.

EXPRESSION AND ADDITION

4. Here is a good Occasion for a Building Good Will letter:

   SITUATION: Paul Caruso was out of the office when Bill, an out-of-town business acquaintance, dropped in to see him. It was just a spontaneous visit. No doubt Bill had actually come to town to see someone else; he found he had a few extra hours; and he decided to spend them with Paul (if possible).

No response at all would not have been rude, but Paul would have missed an opportunity to send a Building Good Will letter. Paul wrote the following letter.

> Dear Bill,
>
> It wasn't fair to miss you on my home territory. Next time, I hope our schedules will mesh.
>
> Cordially,
> Paul
> Paul Caruso

Since Paul felt that he didn't need to mention the Occasion, his letter consisted of only an Expression and an Addition--and in two short sentences.

The Addition, however, was merely polite. Suppose Paul had wanted to be more friendly. Suppose he wants to make certain that Bill knows he's sorry, and that he really wants to see him the next time.

Rewrite the Addition so it will convey this feeling.

Dear Bill,

It wasn't fair to miss you on my home territory. Next time you're in town, let's get together for a drink at least.

(You might also set this Addition off as a separate paragraph, to give it more emphasis.)

A SINCERE TONE

5. A Building Good Will letter can also fail to give pleasure and therefore fail to build good will for the future. Sample A is a notable and actual example of a form letter sent to all new Ph.D.'s by the dean of a large graduate school. (Only the names have been changed!) Although the dean intended to be kind, his letter sounded patronizing and phoney to at least one former student. We'll call this student, Dr. Hugh R. Presuming--husband, father of three, teacher, lecturer, educator. How does the letter strike you?

(A)

Dear Dr. Presuming:

From time to time I have wondered whether those who recently finished their doctoral studies might now welcome an invitation to comment on the quality of their graduate experience at State. I am sure I would learn a great deal from the responding letters. If you have any thoughts you wish to express about the University, the Graduate School, or your individual department or program, I would gratefully receive them and would of course treat them as confidential.

In any case, let me take this opportunity to give you a further warm welcome to the ranks of those who have received their doctoral degrees from this University.

With best wishes,

Sincerely,
Henceforth Foggy
Henceforth Foggy, Dean

You probably felt that Dean Foggy really didn't want to know what the new Ph.D.'s thought about their graduate training. Or maybe he expected them to remember it with nostalgia now that it was a part of their past. Whatever he expected, the tone of Sample Letter A is insincere.

Unlike most of his former classmates, Dr. Presuming decided to call Dean Foggy's bluff; he sent Sample Letter B in response. (This is a somewhat shortened version of the original; and, of course, the names were changed.)

(B)

Dear Dean Foggy:

Thank you for your welcome to the ranks of the degreed.

Thank you also for your invitation to comment on the quality of my graduate experience. I have commented in the past, without invitation. The immediate result was to temporarily solidify the graduate school group in demanding a better system and forcing the faculty into listening. The long-term result was "zilch," as the leaders of the student group graduated and departed for various parts of the world and the faculty became embroiled in yet another political battle for their individual survival.

My comments on my graduate experience are more than just the emotional ones emanating from being a student in the system. They come from years of professional experience in designing instructional systems for the culturally deprived, company executives, and university faculty. In short, educational systems are my business.

Based on my first-hand experience as a graduate student and my professional standards, my summary comment about my graduate experience is

IT STUNK!

In fact, it stunk so bad that it is almost impossible to find a starting point to straighten out the mess. But I have some ideas which I would be glad to share with you if you are really interested. I would accept as a sign of your interest a phone call or a non-form-letter response to this letter.

Sincerely,

Hugh R. Presuming

Hugh R. Presuming, Ph.D

The point of this exchange between Hugh and the dean is that even when the Occasion is appropriate (as it was here), the Building Good Will letter can fail to please if it doesn't sound sincere. Dean Foggy didn't expect any response, and he shouldn't have asked for one--and especially from someone who has had considerable experience in education.

Looking over Dean Foggy's letter again, you will see that it could have been a successful Building Good Will letter if it had consisted of Expression alone. Write a suitable Expression for this situation. You may use the spirit of the Expression in Sample A.

Dear Dr. Presuming:

Congratulations, and welcome to the group of those who have received their doctoral degrees from this University!

Sincerely,
Henceforth Foggy
Henceforth Foggy

OUTLINE FOR A BUILDING GOOD WILL LETTER

6. If you would feel more comfortable jotting down your basic ideas before you actually write a Building Good Will letter, you can prepare this kind of form:

BUILDING GOOD WILL

Occasion:	
Expression:	
Addition:	

When using the outline, you may write either complete sentences, phrases, or just single words--whatever will help you most. (Or don't use the outline at all, if you don't find such outlines helpful.)

Read the following situation, and then Write a Building Good Will letter in response. Try to make your letter short, simple, and sincere. If you wish, you may complete the form above before you actually write.

SITUATION: Miss Ann Rosen of New York Telephone Company is being married to Al Ross, whom she met while they both worked at Bell Telephone Laboratories in New Jersey. Ann is being promoted to a managerial job at Southern Bell in Atlanta, where Al now lives and works. Ann's former boss at Bell Labs wants to write Ann a Building Good Will letter expressing best wishes from other people in the office as well as from himself.

BUILDING GOOD WILL

Occasion:	Wedding bells, supervisory bell, Southern Bell, Southern belle
Expression:	Best wishes from us all.
Addition:	None

Dear Ann,

Wedding bells and the supervisory bell--that's a lot to happen to a soon-to-be Southern belle.

Everyone of us at Bell Labs wishes you and Al a long and happy life together. And good luck on both jobs.

OR

Dear Ann,

Good things come in pairs.

Along with the others in the office, I wish you well in both new jobs.

PRACTICE IN WRITING A BUILDING GOOD WILL LETTER

7. Try writing a Building Good Will letter in response to the following situation.

> SITUATION: An employee's father has died. The boss wants to express his sympathy (and that of the firm) to the employee, Frank Dutton, and to his mother. The boss also wants to tell Frank to take a few days off.

Dear Frank,

We were all very sorry to learn of your father's death. Please express our sympathy to Mrs. Dutton as well.

I would like you to take a few days off so you can be with your family.

8. For practice, write a Good Will letter in response to each of the situations that follow. Remember to make each letter short, simple, and sincere.

SITUATION (a): Janet Delancey in the New York office of a firm won $500 in the state lottery. Paul Guardino in the San Francisco office hears about it and writes Janet to congratulate her. He suggests that she buy him a drink next time he is in New York.

SITUATION (b): Actor Jon Rivera didn't get a part he had wanted in the play Sticks and Bones. His friend sends his regrets and suggests that he try out for a part that suits him in Butterflies Are Free. Jon can call for details.

Compare your letters with the suggestions, and then do the Review of Chapter 4 on page 196.

(a)

Dear Janet,

I heard you won the lottery. Great news.

Next time I'm in town you can buy me a drink.

Sincerely,

Paul

Paul Guardino

(b)

Dear Jon,

Sorry you didn't get to do Sticks and Bones.

I hear they're auditioning for Butterflies Are Free next week. There's a great part in it for you. Why don't you call me for the details.

CHAPTER FIVE

Simplifying Letter Language

How often have you read patterns like the following in business letters? Or worse, how often have you written them yourself? "As per our agreement . . . ." "If I can be of further service . . . ." "Please don't hesitate to call on me . . . ." Or, "I look forward to having the opportunity of serving you in the near future, or at your earliest convenience . . . ."

These are all empty words that do nothing for the message. No matter how mod we get in dress and attitude, most of us sound like pompous Victorians when we write business letters. And, even if all of <u>your</u> letters are <u>short</u>, <u>simple</u>, and <u>sincere</u>, other people will send you such overflowing letters that you'll have to translate as if from a foreign language.

This chapter is for everyone, whether you write or edit stuffy letters or merely have to read them. Perhaps you won't ever learn to drop all of your "businessese"; but you should learn to recognize your more glaringly outmoded expressions. If, after reading this chapter, you do learn to drop some of these expressions, you will have made a big step in writing effective letters.

As usual, you may want to do the Preview to Chapter 5 first (page 197), to see how much stuffiness you now accept.

RECOGNIZING TRITE PATTERNS

1. The style of business letters often falls into a pattern of trite, pompous expressions. One problem is that young people entering old, established businesses imitate the style of their elders. Yet what is desperately needed is a youthful, vigorous style in language.

You will improve your letter-writing style immeasurably by following these few simple guidelines:

(a) If an expression occurs to you too easily, BE CAREFUL! It is probably so familiar because it is overworked. Either think of a simple replacement, or try to drop it altogether.
(b) Don't mention the obvious, like "I read your letter."
(c) When you have said everything you need to say, STOP! This is not an abrupt or rude thing to do. Of course, if you know the person, you may want to add a personal note. But you should never say anything that could dilute the message.

Try an experiment. In each example, the first few words should suggest an overworked pattern. Try to supply the missing words:

(a) for your ______________

(b) we are not in a _________ _________ _________

(c) in the very near ______________

(d) pursuant to our ______________

(e) first and ______________

(f) in this day and ______________

(g) in the normal course _________ _________

(h) permit me to ______________

(i) I thank you _________ _________ _________

(j) We wish to acknowledge _________ _________ _________ _________

- - - - - - - - - - - - - - -

(a) information OR convenience
(b) position to say
(c) future
(d) discussion OR conversation OR agreement
(e) foremost
(f) age
(g) of events OR procedures OR affairs
(h) say OR explain
(i) kindly in advance OR again in advance OR for your attention
(j) receipt of your letter

2. If you were able to complete about six or seven patterns in the preceding exercise, you should be convinced that they are worn out. Dozens and dozens of other similar expressions appear regularly in business letters. The table that follows gives just a few common ones. Read each pattern, and then read its simpler replacement.

OVERWORKED PATTERN	REPLACEMENT
(a) I have (received) your letter	(a) Thank you for your letter
(b) as per our agreement	(b) we agreed as we agreed according to our agreement
(c) at the present writing (time)	(c) now
(d) Please don't hesitate to call	(d) Please call.
(e) at your earliest convenience	(e) soon
(f) Enclosed please find my check.	(f) I have enclosed a check. My check is enclosed.
(g) I have taken the liberty to write	(g) I am writing
(h) for your information	(h) (Drop this altogether!)
(i) I beg to inform you	(i) (Drop this altogether!)
(j) Please feel free to call.	(j) Please call.
(k) according to our records	(k) we find
(l) attached hereto	(l) attached
(m) with regard to your invoice	(m) about your invoice
(n) yours of recent date	(n) your letter of ________
(o) I will send the photograph under separate cover	(o) I will send the photograph (when/maybe how)
(p) the undersigned	(p) I
(q) pending our receipt of your order	(q) when we receive your order

REPLACING TRITE PATTERNS

3. This chapter isn't long enough to cover all the common wordy, outdated patterns. That would take a book--and a very long one. In the remaining exercises in this chapter, however, you will write simple replacements for overworked and empty expressions. Instead of rewriting, you can use a few handy symbols that professional copyeditors and proofreaders use when they need to make changes in writing.

One of the most useful signs is called the delete sign, ⸗, which goes through anything you want to take out. Another is the caret, or ∧ , which is inserted exactly where the added words or punctuation marks belong.

Two capitalization symbols are useful too. To capitalize a letter, you draw the symbol ≡ underneath it. To change a capital letter to a small letter, you draw the symbol / through it. To summarize:

> Delete by drawing ~~~ through the part you don't want. Add by inserting ∧ where the new material belongs. Capitalize a letter by drawing ≡ underneath it. Change a capital to a small letter by drawing / through it.

Here is an example:

> ~~Attached please find~~ my invoice dated June 16, ∧ is attached.

Write simple replacements for the following sentences. Some of the patterns weren't on the list in the preceding exercise, but you will probably recognize them anyway. Be sure your replacements do not change the meaning. You may use the four copyediting symbols shown here (or any of the copyediting and proofreading symbols suggested in Webster's Collegiate Dictionary).

(a) In accordance with your request regarding Mr. Weiss's application, I have read it carefully.

(b) We herewith enclose the letters from the attorney.

(c) We hope this solution is agreeable to your wishes in this matter.

(d) I regret to inform you that I am unable to consider your application for acceptance as of the present writing.

(e) This will acknowledge receipt of your letter of December 12.

(f) Allow me to express my sincere appreciation for sending me your book.

(g) If I can be of further assistance to you in any way, please don't hesitate to call.

(h) I hope you will take the time to look through these photographs.

(i) I am looking forward to the opportunity to address members of your management.

(j) Your assistance was a welcome asset.

(a) As you suggested, ~~In accordance with your request regarding Mr. Weiss's application,~~ I have read ∧ Mr. Weiss's application ~~it~~ carefully.

have d
(b) We ~~herewith~~ enclose the letters from the attorney.

(c) We hope this solution is agreeable. ~~to your wishes in this matter~~

Unfortunately, cannot accept
(d) ~~I regret to inform you that~~ I ~~am unable to consider~~ your application

now.
~~for acceptance as of the present writing~~

I have received
(e) ~~This will acknowledge receipt of~~ your letter of December 12.

Thank you
(f) ~~Allow me to express my sincere appreciation~~ for sending me your book.

Please let me know help further.
(g) ~~If~~ I can ~~be of further assistance to~~ you ~~in any way, please don't hesitate to call~~

(h) I hope you will ~~take the time to~~ look through these photographs.

will be pleased
(i) I ~~am looking forward to the opportunity~~ to address members of your management.

Thank you for help.
(j) ~~Your~~ ~~assistance was a welcome asset~~

CROSSWORD PUZZLE

4. If you like crossword puzzles, you should enjoy this exercise particularly. It is also good practice for everyone. (If you absolutely detest crossword puzzles, you may continue to Exercise 5 right now--provided you realize that you are missing one of life's untaxable pleasures.)

Complete the accompanying puzzle using simple replacements for the long-winded patterns here:

Across

1. I am in receipt of (2 words)
5. In regard to
11. Appended hereto
12. The undersigned
13. According to our records (2 words)
14. Utilization
15. In the negative
16. Anent to
18. Remuneration for services rendered
19. Up until the time of

Down

2. Assistance
3. At the present writing
4. In the affirmative
6. Due to the fact that
7. In the upward direction
8. Notwithstanding
9. Augmented by
10. In the event that
11. Commercial notice
12. I want to say it was a pleasure (2 words)

20. Belonging to
21. In the normal course of events
23. Additionally
25. Under the date of
26. Will you be so kind as to
30. In arrears (over __________)
31. In this day and age
32. Each and all
33. Take it under advisement (3 words)

17. Commenced operating (2 words)
18. With reference to
19. In the direction to
21. Not in the least
22. (They) happen to be in a position to
24. Thusly, in such a fashion
27. At a later date
28. Subsequent to
29. Facile

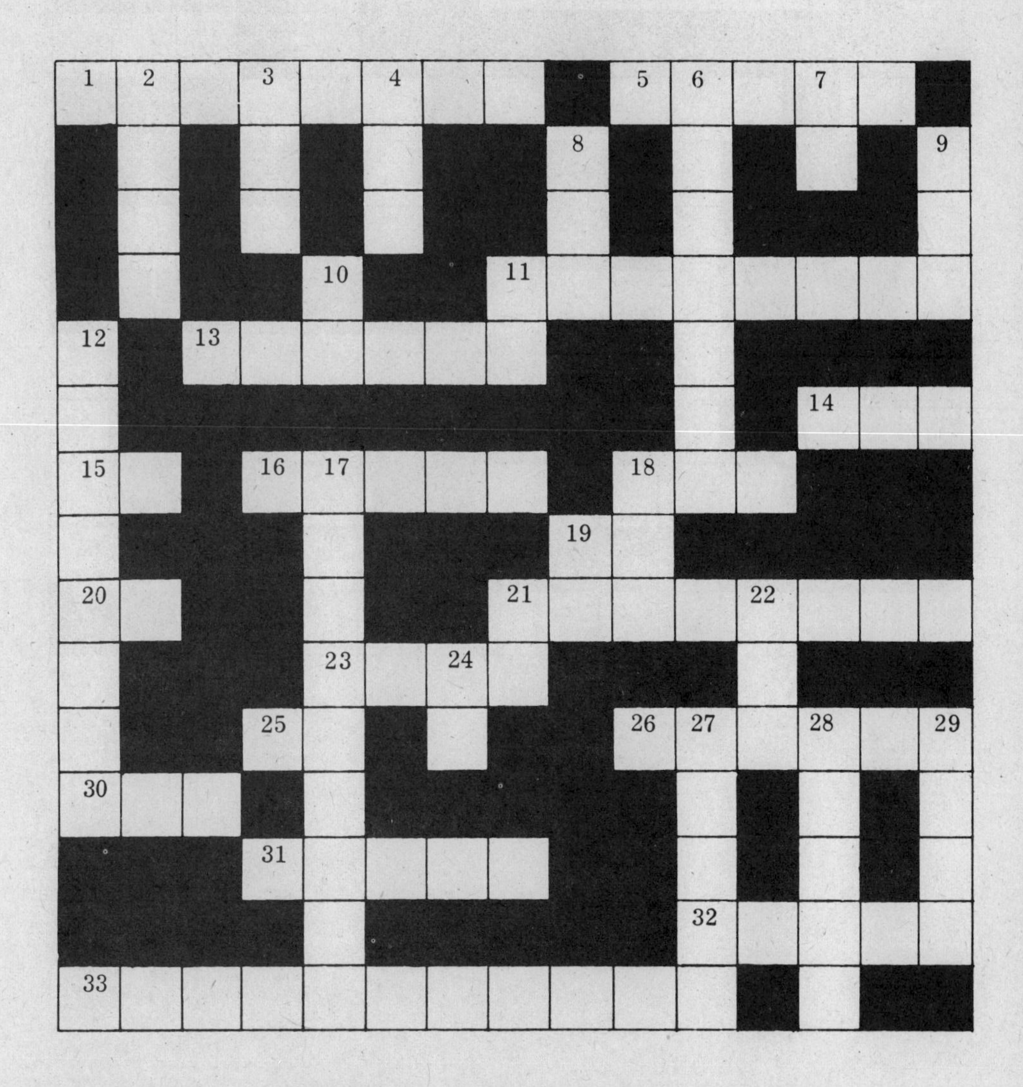

Check your completed puzzle on page 94.

1 T	2 H	A	3 N	K	4 Y	O	U	■	5 A	6 B	O	7 U	T	■
■	E	■	O	■	E	■	■	8 Y	■	E	■	P	■	9 A
■	L	■	W	■	S	■	■	E	■	C	■	■	■	N
■	P	■	■	10 I	■	■	11 A	T	T	A	C	H	E	D
12 I	■	13 W	E	F	I	N	D	■	■	U	■	■	■	■
E	■	■	■	■	■	■	■	■	■	S	■	14 U	S	E
15 N	O	■	16 A	17 B	O	U	T	■	18 F	E	E	■	■	■
J	■	■	■	E	■	■	■	19 T	O	■	■	■	■	■
20 O	F	■	■	G	■	■	21 N	O	R	M	22 A	L	L	Y
Y	■	■	■	23 A	L	24 S	O	■	■	■	R	■	■	■
E	■	■	25 O	N	■	O	■	■	26 P	27 L	E	28 A	S	29 E
30 D	U	E	■	W	■	■	■	■	■	A	■	F	■	A
■	■	■	31 T	O	D	A	Y	■	■	T	■	T	■	S
■	■	■	■	R	■	■	■	■	■	32 E	V	E	R	Y
33 T	H	I	N	K	I	T	O	V	E	R	■	R	■	■

EDITING LETTERS

5. Read and note that the two words in parentheses detract from the letter. Read the letter again without the parenthesized words to see if you agree.

(A)

> Gentlemen:
>
> I would like (to obtain) two extra Admiral Club baggage tags. Can you help me?

This is not an uncommon situation. Many times, perfectly good letters are ruined by a few unnecessary words. This means that they could be saved merely by some careful cutting.

Using the delete sign, do away with the clutter in Sample B. It is actually a reasonable memo underneath the wordiness.

(B)

> TO: All Managers
>
> I have been faced with the assignment of launching a new course in report writing for all of your line supervisors. Right now, I am currently reviewing possible textbooks.
>
> Do you have any suggestions that I might find helpful? I can certainly use anything in the way of your help that you would care to give.

> TO: All Managers
>
> ~~I have been faced with~~ My ~~the~~ assignment is to ~~of~~ launch~~ing~~ a new course in report writing for all

> ~~of your~~ line supervisors. Right now, I am
> ~~currently~~ reviewing possible textbooks.
>
> Do you have any suggestions ~~that I might find helpful~~? I can certainly use ~~anything in the way of~~ your help. ~~that you would care to give~~

6. As you know, unnecessary words are only part of why business letters often need a face lift. The overtired expressions are another reason. Using the copyediting symbols, edit this letter to eliminate unnecessary words and trite patterns.

> Dear Mr. Snow:
>
> I am in receipt of your reply to our recent advertisement.
>
> I have at this writing had the opportunity to review your background of training and experience in relation to our current openings. I regret to inform you that I am unable to encourage you towards association with us. It appears that there are other candidates whom we are considering whose qualifications are more closely related to our specific requirements.
>
> I appreciate your interest in Sanford Insurance Company. I want you to know that I am sorry my reply couldn't be more favorable.
>
> Sincerely yours,
>
> M. T. Sachs
>
> M. T. Sachs

> ~~I am in receipt of~~ Thank you for your reply to our recent advertisement.
>
> I have ~~at this writing had the opportunity to~~ review[ed] your background ~~of training and experience in relation~~ to see if it would be suitable to our current openings. ~~I regret to inform you that I am unable to encourage you towards association with us. It appears that there are~~ Unfortunately, I feel we have other candidates ~~whom we are considering whose~~ with qualifications ~~are more closely related to~~ that meet our ~~specific~~ requirements more closely.
>
> I appreciate your interest in Sanford Insurance Company, and I ~~want you to know that I am sorry my reply couldn't be more favorable~~ wish you luck in finding another job.

7. See what you can do with the following letter to make it modern and readable.

> Dear Mr. Pasco:
>
> This is to acknowledge the receipt of your order of June 10.
>
> According to our records, we find that our invoice of May 10 in the amount of $85 is unpaid as of the present writing. In view of the fact that this account is 30 days in arrears, it would not be in accordance with our rules (which were adopted for the benefit of all our trade) to give you an additional extension of credit.

The condition of your account may have escaped your careful attention. Hence we feel sure that in view of the fact that we have reminded you of it herewith, you will send us your check for the amount of $85. By so doing, you will be conforming to our rules of credit. This will enable us to forward your aforementioned order to the shipping department for immediate processing.

¶ *Thank you for* ~~This is to acknowledge the receipt of~~ your order of June 10.

¶ ~~According to our records,~~ We find*, however,* that our invoice of May 10 *for* ~~in the amoung of~~ $85 is *still* unpaid. ~~as of the present writing. In view of the fact that,~~ *Since* this account is 30 days ~~in arrears,~~ *overdue, we would* ~~it would not be in accordance with~~ *be breaking* our rules ~~(which were adopted for the benefit of all our trade)~~ to ~~give~~ *extend* you *further* ~~an additional extension of~~ credit.

This situation is undoubtedly just an oversight. ~~The condition of your account may have escaped your careful attention. Hence we feel sure that in view of the fact,~~ *Now* that we have reminded you, ~~of it herewith,~~ *we hope* you will send us your check for ~~the amount of~~ $85. ~~By so doing, you will be conforming to our rules of credit.~~ *We will then send* ~~This will enable us to forward~~ your ~~aforementioned~~ order to the shipping department for immediate processing.

8. Here is another stuffy letter. Edit to simplify it.

> Dear Ms. Picky:
>
> I want you to know that we sincerely regret your recent experience with reference to your purchase of Glacé Caramels. We want you to know that we are pleased that you took time out of your busy schedule to bring this matter to our attention.
>
> We wish to assure you that we take every step possible to see that only fresh merchandise reaches our customers. On the rare occasions that this objective is not attained, we are happy to have our customers so inform us.
>
> Under separate cover, we are sending you two boxes of Glacé Caramels. We know you will find they are up to the usual standards you have come to expect from our product. May we also take this opportunity to tell you how much we appreciate your patronage, and to express the hope that you will allow us to serve you for many years in the future.

- - - - - - - - - - - - - -

> ~~I want you to know that~~ We were very sorry to ~~sincerely regret~~
> learn of your
> ~~your recent~~ experience with ~~reference to your~~
> Thank you for
> ~~purchase of~~ Glacé Caramels. ~~We want you to~~
> telling us about it.
> ~~know that we are pleased that you took time out~~

~~of your busy schedule to bring this matter to our attention.~~

~~We wish to assure you that we take every step possible to see that only fresh merchandise reaches our customers. On the rare occasions that this objective is not attained, we are happy to have our customers to inform us.~~

Under separate cover, we are sending you two boxes of Glacé Caramels, which ~~W~~e know you will find ~~they are~~ up to our ~~the~~ usual high standards. ~~you have come to expect from our product. May we also take this opportunity to tell you how much we appreciate your patronage, and to express the hope that you will allow us to serve you for many years in the future.~~

9. Are you ready to decipher the letter that was sent after a ship called the "Clara Ann" collided with a barge in the Mississippi River? Here is a letter that the insurance agents for the ship owners wrote to the agents of the barge owners. It is so completely "businessese" you'll find it hard to believe that the language is really English. Edit this letter to simplify it.

Gentlemen:

We enclose herewith the copies of letters dated December 30, 1971, and February 4, 1972, of Barnes and Storms, the attorneys for the "Clara Ann," in which they are of the opinion that if this case went to trial, the chances are that the "Clara Ann" will be held at fault for the major portion and accordingly they recommend acceptance of settlement offer of the Barge Owners in which the "Clara Ann" will absorb her own damages and will pay to Barge Owners the sum of $5,500 in full settlement.

We will very much appreciate your prompt reply whether you approve Counsel's recommendation in order that we may communicate with them.

Very truly yours,

Compare your editing with the suggestions, and then continue to Chapter 6. If you would like to see how much you have improved your ability to recognize and edit businessese, do the Review of Chapter 5 (page 198) first.

We enclose ~~herewith~~ the copies of letters dated December 30, 1971, and February 4, 1972, of Barnes and Storms. ~~the attorneys for the "Clara Ann," in which~~ As you will see, they ~~are of the opinion~~ believe that if this case went to trial, ~~the chances are that~~ the "Clara Ann" ~~will~~ would probably be held ~~at fault~~ responsible for the major portion of the damages. So, ~~and accordingly~~ they recommend accept~~ance of~~ing the settlement offer of the Barge Owners. ~~in which~~ According to this, the "Clara Ann" will absorb her own damages and will pay ~~to~~ the Barge Owners ~~the sum of~~ $5,500 ~~in~~ as full settlement.

We ~~will~~ would like very much ~~appreciate your prompt reply~~ to know whether you approve ~~Counsel's~~ the recommendation ~~in order that~~ so we ~~may communicate with them.~~ can in turn inform the attorneys.

CHAPTER SIX
Trimming the Hedge

Business letters are often as mysterious as whodunits (but not nearly so interesting), because the writers aren't definite about their facts. They dilute everything they say by using phrases like "it is probable." We say they "hedge." Hedging is not always bad, however. In fact, it is often necessary, since there are times when we can't be absolutely sure about things. The kind of hedging that is objectionable is what business people do when they have nothing to hide, but are just imitating what they have always read.

Sample A is an illustration. As you'll see, this memo describes a decision; but it hedges so much that it actually sounds indecisive.

(A)

> TO: Members of the Training Department
>
> According to several sources, on the average the Guide materials seemed too difficult for most of the average tryout students. It has been decided that the Guide be revised. It is expected that the revision will probably begin next week. It is hoped that new assignments will probably be given at the Friday meeting.

It is probably apparent to you that on the average this memo doesn't actually seem to sound like an announcement of a decision. Sample B illustrates a more positive, decisive way to express the same message.

(B)

> TO: Members of the Training Department
>
> Since many of the tryout students have found our Guide too difficult, we plan to revise. With luck, you will get your assignments at the Friday meeting, and work can begin next week.

This memo hedged only on who made the decision, but not on the decision itself or why it was necessary. The memo is written as if the situation forced the decision; the writer is just doing what the situation demands.

This chapter teaches you how to treat some of those subtle situations that people face when they write business letters. You'll learn

(a) when to be direct, and when to hedge; and
(b) how to do each of these effectively.

Such techniques will help you write business letters that are short, simple, and sincere. You will be asked to copyedit sentences and letters as you did in Chapter 5. Again, instead of rewriting, you can use these four copyediting symbols to point out the changes you want to make:

Symbol	Means
(delete mark)	Delete
∧	Add
≡	Capitalize
/	Make a small letter

As usual, you may turn to the preview of the chapter (on page 199) to find out what you already know about hedging.

ACTIVE AND PASSIVE SENTENCES

1. Before considering the hedge and when and how to use it, let's make sure you know how to build a sentence first.

In conversation and even in writing, a sentence is hard to define. It actually could be any group of words--even a single word. But for the sake of grammar and punctuation, we need a more rigid definition.

A simple sentence (also called a main clause) is said to represent a completed idea. It has an action, which is expressed by a verb. It also has a subject--something or somebody that is always mentioned first. And sometimes an object follows the verb--something or somebody receiving the action.

In an active sentence, the subject of the sentence also does the action. In a passive sentence, the doer of the action follows the verb--or it may not be mentioned at all. However, the doer in a passive sentence is never the subject.

Compare each active sentence here with its passive counterpart. Each subject is underlined once, and each verb is underlined twice. The doer of the action has "D" marked underneath it.

ACTIVE	PASSIVE
(1) I am announcing my retirement. D	(1) My retirement is being announced.
(2) The voters forced them to act. D	(2) They were forced to act by the voters. D
(3) You have won the scholarship. D	(3) The scholarship was won by you. D
(4) We plan to visit the house. D	(4) The house will be visited by us. D

As you see, the active statement is always more direct than the passive statement because we know immediately who did what. The passive statement hedges. In other words, using the passive is one way to hedge; using the active is one way to be direct.

Identify a passive sentence in this list by putting a check mark beside it. Also, in each sentence, underline the subject once and the verb twice. If the doer of the action is there, write a "D" underneath it.

(a) Thank you for your letters._____

(b) Please suggest an alternative plan._____

(c) The decision is a good one._____

(d) He was described as "underprivileged."_____

(e) It was suggested by the voters._____

(f) Your credit cannot be extended further._____

(g) Prices are expected to soar._____

(h) I am sorry to hear about your company's plight._____

(i) He was rejected at the polls._____

(j) References will be given._____

(a) Thank you for your letter._____

(b) Please suggest an alternative plan._____

(c) The decision is a good one._____

(d) He was described as "underprivileged."__✓__

(e) It was suggested by the voters.__✓__

(f) Your credit cannot be extended further.__✓__

(g) Prices are expected to soar.__✓__

(h) I am sorry to hear about your company's plight._____

(i) He was rejected at the polls.__✓__

(j) References will be given.__✓__

MAKING PASSIVES MORE DIRECT

2. You use either active or passive sentences (or both) in a business letter, depending upon whether you want to hedge or be active. Keep in mind that business people tend to hedge by using passives more often than is necessary. If you have this habit too, you should welcome extra practice in changing passives to actives.

You start by looking for the doer of the action. If you find one, state this first. If no doer is mentioned, you'll have to supply one that is reasonable. Try making the passives in the following list more direct. You can follow this example:

We always appreciate
~~Y~~our comments. ~~are always appreciated.~~

(a) Your check was received yesterday.

(b) The taxes have been determined by the county tax assessor.

(c) A certificate is required by the city.

(d) The order was not received by us until October 4.

(e) Your order was delayed by the shipping department.

(f) These students have been badly spoiled by Professor Doyle.

(g) The lawyer was notified.

(h) The children were saved by his quick thinking.

(i) Your signature is requested by the credit department.

(j) The book was written by Roger Kahn.

- - - - - - - - - - - - - - -

(a) ~~Your check was~~ *I* received *your check* yesterday.

(b) ~~The taxes have been determined by~~ the county tax assessor *has determined the taxes.*

(c) ~~A certificate is required by~~ the city *requires a certificate.*

(d) *We didn't receive* the order ~~was not received by us~~ until October 4.

(e) ~~Your order was delayed by~~ the shipping department *delayed your order.*

(f) ~~These students have been~~ *Professor Doyle has* badly spoiled *these students.* ~~by Professor Doyle.~~

(g) *We notified* the lawyer. ~~was notified.~~

(h) ~~The children were saved by~~ his quick thinking *saved the children.*

(i) ~~Your signature is requested by~~ the credit department *requests your signature.*

(j) ~~The book was written by~~ Roger Kahn *wrote the book.*

MAKING LETTERS DIRECT

3. A business letter with many passive statements can make the reader suspect that he is being duped, whether he is or not. As an example, note the tone of this statement:

"Your letter has been received by us."

It sounds as if there were actually something shady about getting a letter!

Unless you want to play down the doer of the action, either because he's not important to your argument or for other reasons, you should make the sentence active. You will sound warmer, more open, and more friendly.

You can use you to refer to the reader, I to represent yourself, and we to indicate your group. Or you can use the third person to be less personal.

Now copyedit this stiff letter to make it sound more natural.

Dear Ms. Tracy:

I have been asked by Mr. Johnson to tell you more about the job.

You would be called by Mr. Johnson his "Girl Friday." This means his letters are to be typed, and his phone has to be answered. Other tasks like filing have to be done by you too.

Are you interested?

Dear Ms. Tracy:

~~I have been asked by~~ Mr. Johnson has asked me to tell you more about the job.

~~You would be called by Mr. Johnson~~ As his "Girl Friday," ~~This means~~ you would type his letters, ~~are to be typed, and~~ answer his phone, ~~has to be answered~~ and do other tasks like filing. ~~have to be done by you too.~~

~~Are~~ If you are interested, could you call me?

WHEN TO HEDGE WITH PASSIVES

4. At times, a direct, active sentence is too blunt, and a passive one would be better. For example, suppose you had to call attention to a customer's error. You wouldn't want to risk antagonizing him, of course. In such a situation, which sentence would you say is better--the active sentence (A) or the passive sentence (B)?

(A)
You didn't enclose your check.

(B)
Your check wasn't enclosed.

You'll probably agree that the passive sentence (B) is more tactful, because it doesn't point the finger of blame so directly. No one enjoys being told he has made an error.

There are other occasions when you would rather not say who did what. So, in writing a business letter, just as in writing anything else, you must first decide on the tone you want. Then you can manipulate the words to convey that tone to your reader.

Suppose a certain Ms. Alvarez didn't show up for an appointment. You want to mention this in your letter to her. Which of the following two sentences (C or D) would be the more tactful way of saying this?

(C)
You evidently failed to mark our appointment on your calendar.

(D)
Our appointment evidently wasn't marked on your calendar.

Which did you choose, the active or the passive?____________________

- - - - - - - - - - - - - - - -

The passive sentence (D) is more tactful.

5. You might want to hedge with a passive when the doer of the action is either obvious or not important to your argument. The following passive sentence is a good example.

(A)
The garbage is picked up twice a week.

Either we don't care who picks up the garbage, or it's obvious.

The active isn't necessary unless we're writing in defense of the garbagemen. In that case, Sample B would be better:

(B)

The garbagemen pick up the garbage twice a week.

Sometimes, letter writers combine both problems: They hedge with a passive, but they also use the word by to introduce the doer. Sample C is an illustration:

(C)

Your hotel room was changed by me yesterday.

There are two ways to improve this sentence. Do you want to make sure everyone knows that you changed the hotel room? If so, you would use the active, as in Sample D.

(D)

I changed your hotel room yesterday.

But if it doesn't matter who did the changing, you might use the passive, as in Sample E.

(E)

Your hotel room was changed yesterday.

For practice, change each of these active sentences to a passive that doesn't mention the doer. The assumption will be that the doer is either obvious or not important to the point or argument you want to make.

(a) The law protects the individual.

(b) You didn't sign your check.

(c) The company will not extend credit to minors.

(d) We didn't expect your call.

(e) The company has issued special warnings.

(f) We have registered several complaints.

(g) The children have worn holes in the rug.

(h) You didn't make the reservations.

(i) The city requires building permits.

(j) We hired ten waiters.

- - - - - - - - - - - - - - - -

(a) ~~The law protects~~ the individual is protected.

(b) ~~You didn't sign~~ your check wasn't signed.

(c) ~~The company will not extend~~ credit won't be extended to minors.

(d) ~~We didn't expect~~ your call was unexpected.

(e) ~~The company has issued~~ special warnings were issued.

(f) ~~We have registered~~ Several complaints have been registered.

(g) ~~The children have worn~~ Holes have been worn in the rug.

(h) ~~You didn't make~~ The reservations weren't made.

(i) ~~The city requires~~ Building permits are required.

(j) ~~We hired~~ Ten waiters were hired.

THERE AS THE SUBJECT

6. Another way to hedge on who did the action is to make the word there the subject of an active sentence. Compare the following two sentences, for example:

(A)
There are good reasons for suspecting him.

(B)
I have good reasons for suspecting him.

Both sentences make the same assertion of suspicion. But Sample A does it without the severe accusation "J'accuse."

The there construction can be used for less important reasons too. For example, it can be used for variety if several sentence subjects are alike. The subject I is a favorite of letter writers, but it is monotonous for their readers. There will relieve this monotony; but of course it shouldn't be used more than once in a short letter.

Improve this memo by starting one of the I sentences with there.

> TO: All Montgomery, Alabama, Workers
>
> As you know, our campaign is in trouble--and I have several theories to explain why.
>
> I have called a meeting for Tuesday (8:00 p.m. in the Elite Cafe) to discuss our depressing problems.
>
> Please come!

- - - - - - - - - - - - - -

> As you know, our campaign is in trouble--
> and ~~I have~~ there are several theories to explain why.
>
> I have called a meeting for Tuesday (8:00 p.m. in the Elite Cafe) to discuss our depressing problems.
>
> Please come!

OR

> As you know, our campaign is in trouble--and I have several theories to explain why.
>
> ~~I have called~~ There is a meeting for Tuesday (8:00 p.m. in the Elite Cafe) to discuss our depressing problems.
>
> Please come!

7. One word of caution about making there the subject of the sentence: It is just deadwood if the sentence already has a subject. For example, do you see any difference in meaning between these sentences?

(A)

There are several courses in law which are already in the catalog.

(B)

Several courses in law are already in the catalog.

You are right if you think these sentences mean exactly the same thing. But Sample A isn't as good as Sample B because it has deadwood--the three underlined words.

Look over each of the hedge sentences below. If the sentence is satisfactory, put a "C" next to it. If it is not a satisfactory hedge, because the sentence already has a subject, delete the deadwood.

(a) There are three different marketing schemes._____

(b) There are several good restaurants that feature Italian food._____

(c) There is considerable interest in his new book._____

(d) There is a small house I found near the beach that sounds perfect._____

(e) There are several students who are flunking math this year._____

(a) C

(b) ~~There are~~ several good restaurants ~~that~~ feature Italian food.

(c) C

(d) ~~There is~~ a small house I found near the beach ~~that~~ sounds perfect.

(e) ~~There are~~ several students ~~who~~ are flunking math this year.

IT AS THE SUBJECT

8. A popular hedge to avoid is making *it* the subject of part of the sentence that doesn't carry the main action. The *it* doesn't refer to anything, as Sample A illustrates:

(A)
It is probable that they will have to go to court.

The direct way to express this thought is as follows:

(B)
They will have to go to court.

As you see, the first four words in Sample A didn't carry the action. However, they do contain a hedge that you may want. If so, you can condense these words to *probably* and insert as follows:

(C)
They will probably have to go to court.

Now there is a hedge, but no deadwood.

Sample D illustrates another kind of hedge carried by a useless *it*:

(D)
It is suggested that they go to court.

This time, we can't just drop the first four words without destroying both the hedge and the meaning. Rearrangements are needed, and so are additions. Samples E and F are illustrations.

(E)
They should go to court.

(F)

The suggestion is that they go to court.

A third kind of hedge introduced by the useless *it* has still other problems. Look at Sample G:

(G)

It is hoped that the discussion will stop.

Most people fix a sentence like that by inserting the word *hopefully*, as in Sample H.

(H)

Hopefully, the discussion will stop.

But many careful writers are offended by this construction. "A discussion can't hope," they say. Sample I is a way out.

(I)

The hope is that the discussion will stop.

When you are tempted to use *hopefully*, also think about who is doing the hoping. This person should be mentioned too, unless the hedge is intentional. For example,

(J)

We hope to finish tomorrow night.

Now the construction with *hopefully* will work too, as Sample K shows.

(K)

Hopefully, we will finish tomorrow night.

For practice, edit these sentences by dropping the *it* part while still preserving the meaning:

(a) It is obvious that we will have to review our records.

(b) It is necessary to remind everyone to complete the time sheet.

(c) It was decided that the parents meet with the teachers next week.

(d) It is hoped that the laws will be different by that time.

(e) It is expected that the news will break this week.

- - - - - - - - - - - - - -

(a) ~~It is~~ obvious ly, ~~that~~ we will have to review our records.

(b) ~~It is necessary to remind everyone~~ Everyone needs a reminder to complete the time sheet.

(c) ~~It was decided that~~ the parents should meet with the teachers next week.

(d) ~~It is~~ The hope~~d~~ is that the laws will be different by that time.

(e) ~~It is expected that~~ the news ~~will~~ is expected to break this week.

SUMMARY OF HEDGES

9. To summarize, business letters sound more sincere, more natural, if the sentences are active. But occasionally we have good reason for hedging. Maybe the direct statement is too harsh; maybe we aren't sure of our facts; or maybe we have mentioned ourselves too often.

Look over this chart on hedges.

Occasion	Solution	Example
(1) To avoid mentioning the doer of action because this is too harsh, the doer is not important, or the doer is obvious.	(a) Use passive, without mentioning doer. (b) Use active, with <u>there</u> <u>is</u> or <u>there</u> <u>are</u>.	(a) ~~I ordered~~ twelve books are ordered. (b) ~~I ordered~~ There are twelve books on order.
(2) To avoid a useless <u>it</u> construction because it is awkward.	(a) Drop the <u>it</u> construction; preserve the hedge by using an adverb or by rearrangements.	(a) ~~It is probably that~~ I probably ordered twelve books. (b) ~~It is hoped~~ The hope is that I ordered twelve books.

The following letter is quite severe. See if you can tone it down somewhat by not casting blame so sharply. You may edit directly on the letter.

> Dear Mr. Overly:
>
> This is the third time I've had to write you about an undeserved charge.
>
> Several months ago, you added a finance charge to my bill even though I had actually paid

my bill on time. I wrote you about it twice, and

I of course didn't pay the extra charge. However,

you have ignored my letters, and you continue to

add a new finance charge each month.

If you don't correct this error within two

weeks, I shall turn in my MONEY CLUB card.

Dear Mr. Overly:

This is the third time I've had to write you

about an undeserved charge.

Several months ago, ~~you added~~ a finance

was added

charge to my bill even though I had actually paid

my bill on time. I wrote you about it twice, and

I of course didn't pay the extra charge. However,

each time *was ignored,*

~~you have ignored~~ my letter~~s~~, and ~~you continue to~~

was added

~~add~~ a new finance charge each month.

is not corrected

If ~~you don't correct~~ this error within two

have to

weeks, I shall turn in my MONEY CLUB card.

EDITING FOR HEDGES

10. Like so many other business letters, this one has many unnecessary hedges. Edit to make the letter sound more natural and more direct.

Dear Mr. Bender:

Yesterday I was given one of your Picca-dillis as a gift. Unfortunately, it was discovered that instructions and recipes were missing.

The Picca-dilli was purchased at Jordan Marsh, Natick, Massachusetts. Naturally, it cannot be used without the instructions.

Please send the instructions and recipe book right away, so that the Picca-dilli can be used. Otherwise, my Picca-dilli will have to be returned.

Dear Mr. Bender:

Yesterday I ~~was given~~ *received* one of your Picca-dillis as a gift. Unfortunately, ~~it was discovered that~~ *the* instructions and recipes were missing.

The Picca-dilli was purchased at Jordan Marsh, Natick, Massachusetts. ~~Naturally it cannot be used without the instructions.~~

> Please send the instructions and recipe book.
>
> ~~right away, so that the Picca-dilli can be used.~~
>
> *I will have to return*
>
> Otherwise, my Picca-dilli. ~~will have to be~~
>
> ~~returned.~~

If you would like to see how much you have learned about hedges and how to use them properly, turn to page 201, and do the Review of Chapter 6. Then consult the Chapter Guide to see where you should go next.

CHAPTER SEVEN
Attending to Details

In nineteenth-century novels, the fate of the heroine may be determined by a very minor detail--a letter, perhaps, which is slipped under the door and goes unnoticed. It is from the hero, of course, and would have spared the little lady a lifetime of misery.

Nowadays, we are too sophisticated to accept such melodrama in our novels. Yet the decisions in the real world rest upon equally tenuous circumstances, and there is truth in the adage that truth is stranger than fiction. Jobs are lost by a misspelled word. An Olympic record is lost by a careless shoelace. A decimal point one place off is the difference between a helpful and a lethal dose of medicine. In short, small things do make a big difference.

This chapter is organized around four areas that can spoil the impression you want your letter to make.

The first area is covered in Section A, called Copyediting for Common Errors. You will learn what you do and don't know about grammar, punctuation, and usage--also, how skillful you are at proofreading. You will learn how to correct your errors or where to get the information or practice you need. You should study this section whether you write, edit, or type letters, because a letter with a spelling or a grammatical mistake reflects badly on everyone who had any share in producing it.

The second area is treated in Section B, called Expressing Numbers. There are several number styles to choose from, but you should know which style is best for getting a particular message across. Knowing the appropriate style will also save on letter production time. In business, a person's time costs money. So, here again, you should study this section whether you write, edit, or type letters.

The third area is covered in Section C, called Dividing Words. Sometimes you do have to divide a word at the end of a line to prevent a ragged, right-hand margin. This section will teach you where to divide the word so the division will make only the smallest possible interruption in the reader's train of thought. Once more, this section is a must if you type or edit letters. However, if all you do is write the letter and never look at the typed product, you can skip Section C.

Finally, the fourth area is handled in Section D, called Typing a Neat Right-hand Margin. It is, of course, for the typist only. It should be a help in teaching you to use the typewriter bell as a clue that the margin line is approaching.

The following chart summarizes this information.

SECTION	COVERS	IT IS FOR
A. Copyediting for common errors	Proofreading and common errors in grammar, punctuation, and usage	Writers, editors, and typists of business letters
B. Expressing numbers	Styles in expressing numbers	Writers, editors, and typists of business letters
C. Dividing words	Dividing a word (if necessary) so it makes the least possible interruption	Editors and typists of business letters
D. Typing a neat right-hand margin	Using the typewriter bell as a clue that the margin line is approaching	Typists of business letters

Since this first section is, in a sense, a preview in itself, it does not have a separate preview as do the other sections. (See pages 202 and 203.) You may do the previews to those sections that will be useful to you. Your performance on a preview will tell you which exercises you need the most and which ones you can lightly review.

A. COPYEDITING FOR COMMON ERRORS

Probably the worst mistake you can make in writing a letter is to misspell the reader's name. How can a "Mr. Krakower" take a letter seriously if it is addressed to a "Mr. Krapower"? His letter had better be good news.

Other spelling errors in letters can be more ridiculous than insulting, as here, for example:

> Dear Madam:
>
> We just received your plague. They did a beatiful job. Please call for same at your earliest convenience.

Can a plaque ever be a plague? If so, should they beatify it?

Before we get to the serious part of this section and you actually copyedit a letter for misspellings and other common errors, you should read the delightful letter that follows. It was inspired by a report that the writer's name was misspelled in an advertisement.

> Dear Mr. Hahn:
>
> Many thanks for your note of 23 March advising me of the imminent misspelling of my name in your Amer. Psychol. advertisement for Irwin Sarason's book. I'm all a-quiver waiting to see whether it's my first name or last name (would you believe both names?) that's gotten loused up. Be assured that this is not the first time that this has happened and it won't be the last time. Accordingly, I have no intention of initiating legal proceedings--(or perhaps I should wait to see how badly it's garbled before I offer such blanket reassurances).
>
> Sincerely,
>
> Emory L. Cowen

A grateful Mr. Hahn responded with an equally delightful letter.

Dear Mr. Cowen:

Your letter of March 27th made my day. (It would have made my week if you had been a Wiley author, but that was too much to hope for.)

I should tell you that you broke a basic rule of the Author's Union by being gracious about a publisher's gaffe. Never, never give an advertising manager an inch. As the Duchess said,

"Speak roughly to your little boy,
And beat him when he sneezes;
He only does it to annoy,
Because he knows it teases."

We spelt your name "Cowan."

Sincerely,

Frederick H. Hahn, Jr.

That didn't end the matter. When the ad finally appeared, Professor Cowen's name had been spelled correctly (with an "e") after all. You can be sure that people in business do worry about misspellings.

1. This section consists mainly of a letter that you will copyedit for errors in spelling, punctuation, grammar, and general rules of good usage. You should not attempt to change the style of the letter. Of course, you may use the four copyediting symbols: ⸙ (delete), ∧ (add), ≡ (capitalize), / (change to small letter).

When you are satisfied with your copyediting, check it against the suggested, copyedited version that follows. In this copyedited version, misspellings have been labeled "sp"; other errors have been numbered. These numbers refer to frequent mistakes that are listed and discussed in the Table of Common Errors (page 124). Any place where your copyediting doesn't agree with the copyedited version, record the number of the error or write "sp" on the blank at the beginning of the line. If you find that you have missed a spelling error, put "sp" on the blank next to the appropriate line. If you have overlooked another kind of error, record the number of that error.

Dear Paul,

(a)____ You'll be interested in something Dan Haggarty and
(b)____ myself have discovered.
(c)____ Due to the recession the goverment wants to give the
(d)____ small busnessman a "shot in the arm". It will, therefore
(e)____ make small loans to worthy individuals who cannot get their
(f)____ loans through the usual channals the banks. Paul between
(g)____ you and I, this is exsiting, it could have a big affect.
(h)____ One of the things that are especially appealing are that
(i)____ I fit the "bill", don't you think? (You do too Paul).
(j)____ Its necessary to incorporate, I think in order to be
(k)____ eligable. I'm not sure, all the data is at the office,
(l)____ (where I rarely am these days) and its so late I can't
(m)____ think straight.
(n)____ Why don't you call me at American Telephone and
(o)____ Telegraph Company? I'll be there everyday next week.
(p)____ AT&T is close to your place, isn't it? Maybe we can meet
(q)____ for lunch Wedsnesday is best for me and discuss it farther.
(r)____ A number of interesting places is near there that I
(s)____ can recommend. One of the places on the North side of
(t)____ John Street are featuring southren food. (That's my
(u)____ favorite).
(v)____ By the way the recession has effected our household
(w)____ seriously. (It's affects are every where I suppose).
(x)____ According to an articel I read in The New York Times,
(y)____ (called Recession Low Notes) the situation will improve
(z)____ soon. I hope so. We'll talk Wedesday.

Dear Paul,

(a) You'll be interested in something Dan Haggarty and

(b) myself have discovered.

(c) Due to the recession the goverment wants to give the

(d) small busnessman a "shot in the arm". It will therefore

(e) make small loans to worthy individuals who cannot get thier

(f) loans through the usual channals the banks. Paul between

(g) you and I, this is exsiting, it could have a big affect.

(h) One of the things that are especially appealing are that

(i) I fit the "bill", don't you think? (You do too, Paul).

(j) Its necessary to incorporate, I think in order to be

(k) eligable. I'm not sure; all the data is at the office,

(l) (where I rarely am these days) and its so late I can't

(m) think straight.

(n) Why don't you call me at American Telephone and

(o) Telegraph Company? I'll be there everyday next week.

(p) AT&T is close to your place isn't it? Maybe we can meet

(q) for lunch Wedsnesday is best for me and discuss it farther.

(r) A number of interesting places is near there that I

(s) can recommend. One of the places on the North side of

(t) John Street are featuring southren food. (That's my

(u) favorite).

(v) By the way the recession has effected our household

(w) seriously. (It's affects are every where I suppose.)

(x) According to an articel I read in The New York Times,

(y) (called Recession Low Notes) the situation will improve

(z) soon. I hope so. We'll talk Wedesday.

Evaluation

How did you do? Start by counting the spelling errors you missed. If there were many of them, you should take the warning and learn to proofread more carefully. If you missed several other errors through careless proofreading, perhaps from now on you should first read each letter by yourself; then ask someone else to read it to you. Often this double check is a good way to catch errors you hadn't noticed.

Each number in parentheses refers to an entry in the Table of Common Errors below. Check out everything you missed. Perhaps the entry in the table will refresh your memory about a point of grammar. usage, or punctuation that you have forgotten.

The table entry may not be a complete-enough explanation for you, however. Or, perhaps, you just need some practice. If so, you can study Clear Writing, by Marilyn B. Gilbert, published by John Wiley & Sons, Inc., in 1972. This book will give you step-by-step instruction in some of the basic principles of constructing and punctuating sentences correctly.

You may also need a reference book. One of the best is Words into Type, by Margaret E. Skillin, Robert M. Gay, and other leading authorities. The revised edition was published by Appleton-Century-Crofts in 1964.

And need we mention that a dictionary--a recent edition--is indispensable, and that a thesaurus is also very helpful?

This section can merely point out some of your problems. It can by no means correct any but the minor ones. The rest is up to you.

Table of Common Errors

2. In the following chart, the situation or common error is in the first column. The rule or explanation is found next to this, and an example is given last. Each entry number corresponds to an error noted in the copyedited letter on page 123.

IF	THEN	EXAMPLE
(1) myself is used.	(1) it must be preceded by I; in that case, myself is often unnecessary except for emphasis.	(1) You should know Jean and (myself) I will be working hard.

IF	THEN	EXAMPLE
(2) due to is used,	(2) it must be an adjective and not a preposition.	(2) ~~Due to~~ Because of inflation, we had to cut our expenditures. BUT Our problems are due to inflation.
(3) a short introductory phrase is used,	(3) it is set off by a comma if it is extra information; it is not set off if it is essential.	(3) Because of the heat the crowd left early. BUT By the way, the crowd left early.
(4) a comma or period is used with a closing quote mark.	(4) the comma or period goes inside the closing quote. A semicolon or a colon goes outside.	(4) We listened to "America the Beautiful." BUT We listened to "America the Beautiful": It was nice.
(5) therefore is used as an adverb, but not to link clauses,	(5) it is set off by commas if the reader should pause; otherwise, it is not set off.	(5) We are, therefore, responsible for him. OR, BETTER, We are therefore responsible for him.

IF	THEN	EXAMPLE
(6) a special description interrupts the flow of the sentence.	(6) it is not set off by itself if it narrows the meaning and makes it more specific;	(6) The book Rebecca was also a movie.
	it is set off by commas if it is the usual nice-to-know, extra information;	The book, a novel, was his first success.
	it is set off by dashes if it could use some emphasis;	He went to the usual source--the bank.
	it is set off by a colon if it could use some drama;	He went to the usual source: the bank.
	it is set off in parentheses if it could be deemphasized.	He went to the usual source (the bank).
(7) the writer addresses someone directly,	(7) the name is set off by commas.	(7) You know, Paul, I like you.
(8) I is used,	(8) it must be a subject; me is used only as an object of a verb or of a preposition.	(8) This is between you and me.

IF	THEN	EXAMPLE
(9) two main clauses are joined without a linking adverb,	(9) a semicolon must be used to join them.	(9) This is very cruel; it could injure him for life.
(10) affect is used,	(10) it must be a verb that means "to in-influence"; the word effect is a noun meaning "result," or a verb meaning "to bring about."	(10) Heat affects every-one. BUT The heat has a bad effect on me.
(11) one is the subject of the sentence,	(11) the verb must be singular.	(11) One of my students is a concert pianist.
(12) a sentence is enclosed in paren-theses and is set off by itself,	(12) it begins with a capital letter and ends with a period that goes inside the closing parenthesis.	(12) (He asked her too late.)
(13) its is used, or it's,	(13) it's is a short form for it is; its is the possessive form meaning "belonging to it."	(13) It's too late. OR Its wing is hurt.

IF	THEN	EXAMPLE
(14) a minor sentence interrupts the flow of the main thought,	(14) set if off from the rest of the sentence by commas, dashes, or parentheses.	(14) This is, I suppose, fun. This is--I suppose--fun. This is (I suppose) fun.
(15) a group of words is enclosed in parentheses and is also a part of a main sentence,	(15) don't put any punctuation before the opening parenthesis; put it after the closing parenthesis instead.	(15) I asked Paul (the oldest boy), and he agreed.
(16) two main clauses are joined by the linking word and, but, or yet,	(16) join them by a comma before the linking word.	(16) I am sorry, but you can't go.
(17) a sentence begins with an abbreviation,	(17) recast it so the abbreviation comes elsewhere.	(17) The A & P is my favorite supermarket.
(18) a parenthesized sentence is enclosed within another sentence.	(18) don't start it off with a capital letter, and don't end it with a period.	(18) This is Mary (she's my oldest sister); you two will get along just fine.
(19) farther is used.	(19) it refers to a distance; further means "in addition," or "more."	(19) I walk farther than you. BUT Let's discuss this further.

IF	THEN	EXAMPLE
(20) number is the subject of the sentence,	(20) use a plural verb with a number; use a singular verb with the number.	(20) A number of us are going. BUT The number of us who are going is slowly dwindling.
(21) a direction is used,	(21) capitalize it if it is actually a direction; don't capitalize it if it refers to a place.	(21) He lives on the south side of town. BUT John is from the South.
(22) it is the title of a publication,	(22) underline (italicize) a title of a book or paper. Set off in quotes a title of a short publication like a poem, or a song, or an article.	(22) I read The New Yorker--a fine magazine. BUT I read the article "Marriage Means to Die."
(23) it is a long introductory phrase or clause.	(23) set it off by a comma.	(23) According to everything I've ever read, you're wrong.

Now let's get back to business letters. You may either continue to Section B, Expressing Numbers, or refer to the Chapter Guide to see where you might want to go next.

B. EXPRESSING NUMBERS

Many business matters sooner or later lead to a contract: a promise to deliver something on a specified date, at a specified time, and for a specified sum of money. The transaction involves many numbers, and any business letter associated with such a transaction has many numbers too. Should we use figures? Should we spell out the words? These are not weighty questions, but finding the answers can waste valuable production time.

There are several different number styles to choose from. But unless you pick one style beforehand, you'll surely be inconsistent when you write. And consistency is important, if only because switching from one number style to another in the same letter or document can distract the reader. It can even encourage the reader to give the switch in style a significance it doesn't deserve.

The most common number style is the so-called figure style, in which figures are used for 10 and anything higher. Next in popularity is the word style, in which most numbers are spelled out.

The right style depends on the kind of writing. As a guide, the figure style is better for technical materials and for business reports and letters with many numbers, because the figures are easier for the reader to grasp than words. For nontechnical materials, or executive letters that generally have only a few numbers, the word style is better because we tend to avoid symbols like figures in more formal correspondence.

As you may have noticed, the word style is used in the teaching portions of Communicating By Letter, because the numbers there are incidental and infrequent. But the figure style is used whenever it is appropriate in the sample letters.

General Rules

1. In the figure style for numbers, the general rule is to spell out any number from one through nine, but to use figures for 10 and any higher number. For example,

(A)

He gave only four lectures last year.

He gave only 12 lectures last year.

In the word style for numbers, the general rule is to spell out all numbers that are only one or two words. (A hyphenated number like twenty-one counts as only one word.) This means that all numbers from one through one hundred are spelled out--and many higher numbers too. For example,

(B)

They sold ninety-nine tickets.

They sold fifteen hundred tickets.

Ask the fifty-five million people who buy it.

They sold 101 tickets.

As you see in Samples A and B, the general rules are simple. The only time you might wonder what to do is in a set of related numbers when you would normally express some numbers as figures and spell out the rest. To show they are all related numbers, you should express all of them alike. The practice is to use figures for all numbers if only one of them should have been a figure anyway. This is the practice regardless of style. As an example, using figure style we get:

(C)

I interviewed 13 women and 5 men.

I invited 128 men and 96 women.

These same examples in word style are as follows:

(D)

I interviewed thirteen women and five men.

I invited 128 men and 96 women.

Keep in mind that the figure style is better in most business letters and technical reports. But the word style is better in nontechnical materials and executive-level correspondence.

Edit the numbers in the following sentences according to one of these styles or both. (You may want some practice using both number styles.) Write "F" for "Figure" or "W" for "Word" beside each sentence if the number is expressed incorrectly, and also change the number in the sentence. If the number is expressed correctly, write "C."

(a) He expected 2 new shipments this week._____

(b) He ordered 1,200 pairs of hose last year._____

(c) He bought 128 cases of whiskey: 50 cases of vodka, 50 cases of gin, and 28 cases of bourbon._____

(d) They need 500 more invitations._____

(e) He ordered 75 cases of whiskey: 50 cases of vodka, 20 cases of gin, and 5 cases of rum. _____

If you used the figure style:

(a) W two ^

(b) C

(c) C

(d) C

(e) C

If you used the word style:

(a) W ~~2~~ two new shipments

(b) W ~~1,200~~ twelve hundred pairs

(c) C

(d) W ~~500~~ five hundred more invitations

(e) W ~~75~~ seventy-five cases... ~~50~~ fifty cases... ~~20~~ twenty cases... ~~5~~ five cases...

Exceptions

2. There are of course exceptions to the general rules. But, as you'll see, each exception is supported by a reason: Usually this reason is to make the number easier for the reader to grasp.

One such exception involves a round number in the millions or billions that can't be said in one or two words. We write 524 billion rather than 524,000,000,000 because it is easier to grasp.

Of course, an exact number in the millions or billions is always expressed in figures, and again because it is easier to grasp. Can you imagine writing out 524,786,982,435? It would probably take up a full line.

A second exception to the general rule is a decimal. Obviously, 0.66 is easier to grasp than sixty-six hundredths. The zero is used so the reader will be sure to note the decimal point.

A fraction is another exception. If it is a mixed number--that is, a whole number plus a fraction--it is always in figures. Spelling out 46-3/4, for example, would be ridiculous. But when the fraction is a simple one, we spell it out if we can use one or two words. Otherwise, we express it as a figure. For example, we would write three-fourths but put 99/100 in figures.

Measurements are another exception. Since they usually have some technical significance, they are expressed as figures. For example, 2 feet is easier to grasp than two feet.

Sums of money are still another exception. Figures are used for exact amounts of money. Again, $560 is easier to grasp than five hundred and sixty dollars. Similarly, 25 cents is easier to grasp than twenty-five cents. But we have to spell out an indefinite amount like this: He is responsible for several thousands of dollars.

Another exception is a number that starts a sentence. We always spell out this number and any related number. For example, we would write: One hundred and one men and ninety-two women belong. Another way to deal with this situation is to recast the sentence in some way so the number is no longer at the beginning. The same sentence could be written like this: In all, 101 men and 92 women belong; or, the total number belonging is 101 men and 92 women.

A final exception is a number that represents a number. It is always a figure. For example: His score was 75; or, you'll find that in Figure 6, on page 6.

From what you have learned here so far, would you say that the numbers in the following sentence are expressed in the best way possible?

The vote was eight to one.

If you don't think so, how would you express these numbers so they are immediately more meaningful? ______________________________

____

- - - - - - - - - - - - - - -

A better way to write the sentence is: The vote was 8 to 1.

3. This table summarizes all the exceptions we have considered so far. Look them over.

EXCEPTION	USE THE FIGURE	SPELL OUT
(1) A number in the millions or billions that needs more than two words:	(1) for an exact number, like 234,567,890	(1) the word million or billion in a round number, like 345 million
(2) A decimal:	(2) 0.663	
(3) A fraction:	(3) for a mixed number, like 33% for a simple fraction that needs more than two words, like 60/80	(3) a simple fraction that needs only one or two words: three-fifths
(4) A measurement:	(4) 3 inches	

EXCEPTION	USE THE FIGURE	SPELL OUT
(5) Money:	(5) for an exact amount, as follows: $456 and 50 cents	(5) an indefinite amount like this: He bought several hundreds of dollars' worth of food.
(6) A number that begins a sentence, and also any related number used with it:	(6) and recast the sentence so the number no longer starts: About 20 to 30 percent of the people use it.	(6) both numbers, like this: Twenty to thirty percent of the people use it.
(7) A number that represents a number:	(7) His score is 82.7. The vote is 2 to 1. Figure 2 is on page 45.	

Now apply the exceptions to the following sentences. But watch out! Some may follow the general rule. Pick a style, either figure style or word style or both, and identify the style as "F" for "Figure" or "W" for "Word." If the number isn't expressed correctly according to the style you have chosen, edit the sentence. Otherwise, write "C" for "Correct."

(a) It cost $950,000,000._____

(b) The vote is 99 to 67._____

(c) The tea cost 89¢._____

(d) I invited 12 women and 13 men._____

(e) 4 or 5 people are here._____

(f) He invited 50 men and 75 women._____

(g) He called 3 times._____

(h) It's about 7/8 of the class._____

(i) It is .6._____

(j) A kilogram is 2.2 pounds._____

If you used the figure style:

(a) _____ $950 ~~,000,000~~ million

(b) C

(c) _____ ~~89¢~~ 89 cents

(d) C

(e) _____ ~~4~~ Four or ~~5~~ five

(f) C

If you used the word style:

(a) _____ $950 ~~,000,000~~ million

(b) C

(c) _____ ~~89¢~~ 89 cents

(d) _____ ~~12~~ twelve women and ~~13~~ thirteen men

(e) _____ ~~4~~ four or ~~5~~ five

(f) _____ ~~50~~ fifty men and ~~75~~ seventy-five women

(g) ____ 3 three (g) ____ 3 three

(h) ____ 7/8 seven-eighths (h) ____ 7/8 seven-eighths

(i) ____ 0.6 (i) ____ 0.6

(j) C (j) C

Ordinals

4. Ordinals (that is, numbers like first and third) are special. The general rule is to spell them out if they are only one or two words long; otherwise, use ordinal figures. For example:

This is the 133rd time I mentioned it.

This is the thirty-third time I mentioned it.

One common use of ordinals is in numbered street names. Here, we spell out the names of streets up through Tenth. But we use ordinal figures for the higher ones. For example:

John Wiley is on Third Avenue.

She lives at 423 40th Street.

The reason for the th is so the reader doesn't confuse the house number and the street name. The th isn't needed if some direction interrupts, as here:

It is on 424 West 40 Street.

Ordinals also occur in dates. If the day precedes the month or if it stands alone, we either use the ordinals or the words--depending on the style we have chosen for the other numbers. For example:

Figure style: the 21st of May

Word style: the twenty-first of May

But if the day follows the month, we use just the regular figures. (They are called cardinal numbers.) It is correct to write May 21, not May 21st.

Correct the following ordinals, if necessary. As before, you may use either the figure style or the word style or both.

(a) 31 31 Street

(b) 406 2nd Avenue

(c) May 25th

(d) the 5th time

(e) the 6th of June

(f) the 99th time

(a) 33 31st Street

(b) 406 ~~2nd~~ Second Avenue

(c) May 25~~th~~

(d) the ~~5th~~ fifth time

(e) Correct in figure style; in word style, the ~~6th~~ sixth of June

(f) the ~~99th~~ ninety-ninth time

Practice

5. Edit the numbers in the following sentences for practice. First identify the style you're using. Write "F" for "Figure" and "W" for "Word" if a number isn't expressed correctly in that style. Write "C" for "Correct."

(a) He counted 12,000 words in the first story and 1,500 in the other._____

(b) He read for 5 more parts._____

(c) He weighs 44 pounds._____

(d) The store is on 24 4th Avenue.

(e) 40 or 50 envelopes are enough._____

(f) He organized 4 clubs in New Orleans and 15 in Miami._____

(g) It cost 75¢._____

(h) This is the 2nd time I've seen the movie._____

(i) As of January 1st, 1972, we have had 208,000,000 Americans._____

(j) Her birthday is the 26th of January._____

Check your answers, and then you may do the Review (page 204) to see what you have learned. You should either continue to Section C, on Dividing Words, or check the Chapter Guide to see where you might want to go next.

If you used the figure style:

(a) C

(b) _____ ~~5~~ five

(c) C

(d) _____ 24 ~~4~~ Fourth Avenue

(e) _____ ~~40~~ Forty or ~~50~~ fifty

(f) C

If you used the word style:

(a) _____ ~~1,200~~ twelve hundred words ~~1,500~~ fifteen hundred

(b) _____ ~~5~~ five

(c) C

(d) _____ 24 ~~4~~ Fourth Avenue

(e) _____ ~~40~~ Forty or ~~50~~ fifty

(f) _____ ~~4~~ four clubs ~~15~~ fifteen

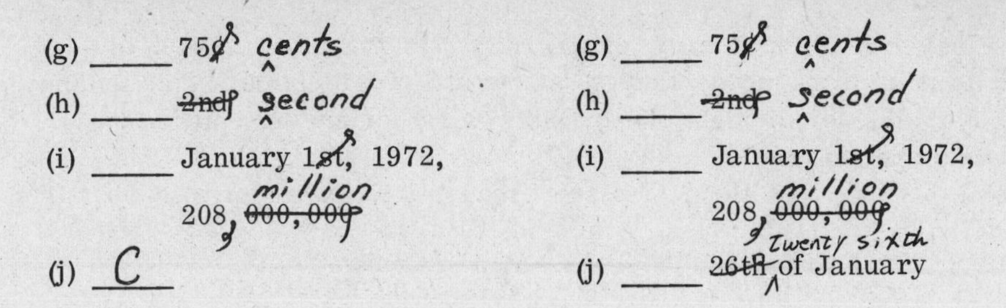

C. DIVIDING WORDS

In New York, "Con Ed" is the name given to the City's utility company ("Consolidated Edison"), which is blamed for many of New York's pollution problems. It is also much criticized for its high utility rates and its difficulties in coping with special situations, like very hot days when people consume super amounts of energy.

With this background, perhaps you can comment on the following notice that appeared in the news index of The New York Times. Would you say the typesetter was trying to tell New Yorkers something?

> Otto M. Manz, Jr., ex-Con
> Edison executive, Page 32

On first reading, you might wonder why the death of an "ex-con" is important enough to warrant mention in the news index. On second reading, you might understand. Now you're blaming the typesetter: Was it pure malice or just his peculiar sense of humor? On third reading, however, you decide that a typesetter has so many words to divide that he probably didn't notice anything strange.

In typing a letter, you have the same problem: maintaining an even right-hand margin with words that come in all sizes, from a to antidisestablishmentarianism. In this section, you'll learn the guidelines for any necessary word divisions.

One-Syllable Sound

1. If we just wanted to make sure that a business letter was as easy to read as possible, we would never divide a word. But we do divide words, because we care what the letter looks like, and we like to see a fairly even right-hand margin.

To make the division easy for the reader to grasp, we always divide a word as it is pronounced--that is, at the end of a syllable. This means that we would never divide a one-syllable word, or a word that is pronounced as one syllable.

Read this example aloud, and see if you can tell what might happen if we did:

> Unfortunately, the insurance company hasn't drop-
> ped the matter. They are still investigating it.

Did you start to read dropped as a two-syllable word? If so, the point was made.

Other places where we never make divisions are in contractions, short words of five letters or less, and abbreviations. We also never divide a word unless we can leave at least two letters. Some examples of words we don't divide are about, doesn't, into, Ph.D, and I.Q.

Put a check mark beside each word that you wouldn't divide:

(a) again _____	(f) drake _____	(k) bland _____
(b) summit _____	(g) report _____	(l) marked _____
(c) corner _____	(h) smiled _____	(m) oleo _____
(d) I'll _____	(i) pencil _____	(n) bleak _____
(e) leaped _____	(j) joke _____	(o) don't _____

(a) ✓	(f) ✓	(k) ✓
(b) _____	(g) _____	(l) ✓
(c) _____	(h) ✓	(m) ✓
(d) ✓	(i) _____	(n) ✓
(e) ✓	(j) ✓	(o) ✓

Root Words

2. As you know, the dictionary shows how words are separated into syllables. If you're really stuck about how to divide a word, you can always consult a dictionary (or one of those special books that give word divisions). This lesson won't attempt to teach you every possible rule about word divisions. (That would be a book in itself.) Here we just want to help you out by giving you a theory about most of them. This theory won't help you divide every word you run into, but it will usually work.

The theory is that you want the division to be simple for the reader to follow; and you don't want to interrupt his reading, if you can help it. An important guideline is to divide the word so that one of the parts that is left will suggest what the whole word might be.

As an example, suppose we wanted to divide the word assignment. Since it is a three-syllable word (say it aloud to test this), we have two choices: to divide after as or after sign. Let's compare these divisions. Which is easier for you to read?

(A)
Since this is your first assignment, I suggest that you...

(B)
Since this is your first assignment, I suggest that you...

The division in Sample B was easier, wasn't it? The reason is that assign gives you the gist of the meaning. We call a word like assign a root word, since it means something when it stands alone; however, this meaning can be modified somewhat by the addition of an ending or a beginning. If you want to divide a word that has a root word inside it, you should try to keep this root intact. That way, the reader will get the gist of the word being divided, and the division won't disturb his reading.

Sometimes the root word is hidden because the e (which was silent) is dropped when the ending is added. But we still follow the rule of keeping the root word intact, and we divide at the ending. For example:

flam-ing AND chang-ing

Try making some divisions. Draw a vertical line at the best dividing point, like this:

wander|ing

(a) bracing
(b) performance
(c) terrorize
(d) unconscious
(e) pretest
(f) framing
(g) consignment
(h) advertisement
(i) imbalance
(j) firebug

(a) brac|ing
(b) perform|ance
(c) terror|ize
(d) un|conscious
(e) pre|test
(f) fram|ing
(g) consign|ment
(h) advertise|ment
(i) im|balance
(j) fire|bug

Other Hints

3. Here are a few more hints. First, if the word is hyphenated, you should divide at the hyphen. Remember the example of "ex-Con Edison." The typesetter could have avoided all the confusion by heeding a simple rule and dividing after ex.

You should also divide a double consonant unless it would mean breaking the root word. For example:

clas-sic   thin-ner   swim-ming

BUT

mess-ing

And you should divide two consonants that stand between two vowels--unless this division would interrupt a root word. Thus:

abun-dant   BUT   accept-ance

Next, you divide two vowels if you do pronounce them separately. As an example:

immedi-ately   BUT   beau-tiful

There are also some endings that are never divided. Examples are -ceous, -cial, -cion, -scious, -geous, -gion, -gious, -sial, -tial, -tion, -tious, and -sion. You probably won't remember these, but you can look them up. You can also look up words ending in -ible and -able when you want to divide them, because sometimes you can divide this ending and sometimes you can't.

Try to apply some of these hints to the following words. Draw a vertical line to show where you would make the division.

(a) referring
(b) blessing
(c) happening
(d) hindering
(e) pouting
(f) flaunting
(g) special
(h) self-control
(i) burdening
(j) viable
(k) personnel
(l) pliable
(m) expiate
(n) contented
(o) right-hand

(a) refer|ring
(b) bless|ing
(c) happen|ing
(d) hinder|ing
(e) pout|ing
(f) flaunt|ing
(g) spe|cial
(h) self-|control
(i) burden|ing
(j) vi|able
(k) person|nel
(l) pli|able
(m) expi|ate
(n) content|ed
(o) right-|hand

Summary

4. Let's summarize what we've said about good dividing points. When the word doesn't have a root word, and yet we can divide it since it is more than one syllable and longer than five letters, the following is handy:

DIVIDE	EXAMPLE
(1) a double consonant	(1) refer-ring
(2) two consonants between two vowels	(2) whis-per
(3) two vowels pronounced separately	(3) appropri-ate

If these hints don't help, just remember to divide a two-syllable word after the first syllable. And divide a three-syllable word, or longer, after the vowel. For example:

particu-lar AND sepa-rate

Now practice all the guides and hints you've learned. Draw a vertical line at the best dividing point. But write "C" if the word can't be divided.

(a) vertical
(b) horizontal
(c) blending
(d) spacious
(e) culminate
(f) report
(g) plucked
(h) spendthrift
(i) porcupine
(j) friendship
(k) pickl|ing
(l) self|-expression
(m) plantation
(n) penalize
(o) blasted

(a) verti|cal
(b) horizon|tal
(c) blend|ing
(d) spa|cious
(e) culmi|nate
(f) re|port
(g) C
(h) spend|thrift
(i) porcu|pine
(j) friend|ship
(k) pickling
(l) self|-expression
(m) planta|tion
(n) penal|ize
(o) blast|ed

Practice

5. Divide these words. Draw a vertical line at what is probably the best dividing point; write "C" if the word can't be divided.

(a) conversation
(b) flunked
(c) mansion
(d) pencil
(e) interrupt
(f) vice-president
(g) blown
(h) capacity
(i) bleeding
(j) control
(k) congratulations
(l) flagrant
(m) principle
(n) pleasing
(o) backward
(p) produce
(q) spinning
(r) compulsive
(s) placing
(t) grown

(a) conversa|tion
(b) C
(c) man|sion
(d) pen|cil
(e) inter|rupt
(f) vice-|president
(g) C
(h) capac|ity
(i) bleed|ing
(j) con|trol
(k) con|gratulations
(l) fla|grant
(m) prin|ciple
(n) pleas|ing
(o) back|ward
(p) pro|duce
(q) spin|ning
(r) com|pul|sive
(s) plac|ing
(t) C

Dividing Groups

6. You should also try to keep certain word groups intact to avoid interrupting the reader unnecessarily. For example, the page and the number are better read together, as are the month and the day, the month and the year, the title and the last name, and a number with a unit of measure. The following examples should not be divided:

page 5 January 1973 January 4

Mr. Jones 2 gallons

Sometimes you do have to divide the longer word groups, however. Still, if you keep in mind that your main concern is making things easy for the reader, you'll be able to handle these divisions too. For example, which would be easier to read, Sample A or Sample B?

(A)	(B)
February 12, 1973	February 12, 1973

The reader certainly gets more information from Sample A than he does from B, and so A is better here.

What about the following situation? Which would be easier for the reader, Sample C or Sample D?

(C)	(D)
516 Parker Avenue	516 Parker Avenue

Again, the first choice--C--is better because the reader isn't left wondering what an isolated number is going to refer to.

You may also divide names of places between the city and the state, and names of persons between the first name plus the middle initial and the last name.

From these guidelines, can you suggest a good dividing point for this name plus title?

The Honorable Richard H. Henning

The Honorable Richard H. | Henning

(This division would give the reader a clue about who The Honorable is.)

Practice

7. Now suggest a good dividing point for each word or group of words. As usual, you can draw a vertical line at the point of the division. If you cannot divide the word or expression, you can just write "C."

(a) gallon

(b) 3 gallons

(c) January 15

(d) January 15, 1973

(e) Chester E. Leef

(f) astronaut

(g) nine times

(h) perfect

(i) page 3

(j) Dr. Sanders

(k) Cleveland, Ohio

(l) 212 West 81 Street

Check your answers, and then try the Review of this section on page 204. Either continue on to Section D, Typing a Neat Right-Hand Margin, or check the Chapter Guide to see where you want to go from here.

(a) gal|lon

(b) C

(c) C

(d) January 15,|1973

(e) Chester E.|Leef

(f) astro|naut

(g) C

(h) per|fect

(i) C

(j) C

(k) Cleveland,|Ohio

(l) 212 West 81|Street

D. TYPING A NEAT RIGHT-HAND MARGIN

Perhaps the typist's hardest job is to make a neat right-hand margin. A ragged edge looks sloppy and makes the whole letter look sloppy too.

Many typists fail to make neat right-hand margins because they return the carriage too soon after the bell rights. What they need to learn is how much more they can type before they will reach the outer limit.

You're going to learn how to make this simple judgment now.

Judging Ten Spaces

1. As you know, a good right-hand margin comes as close to the outer limit as possible, and it doesn't go beyond.

Setting the margins is the first step. From there, you can rely on the typewriter bell to warn you that only ten spaces* remain before you

*Your typewriter might allow more than ten spaces after the bell. If so, you can make the necessary adjustments. The point of this lesson is just to give you the idea of how to make the judgment. You would of course have to practice on your own typewriter.

reach the outer limit. And that includes the space you are on just as the bell rings. To get a neat margin, you must try to fill these spaces up. But you don't want to spend time in actually counting them. This means you should learn to estimate instead.

Study these examples to get some notion of what you can type in ten spaces.

```
                                       Bell
                                        ↓
As I pointed out in my letter of March 1, we will|
                                        ↓
About the only information we need for our report|
                                        ↓
We can process your order of June 1, 1972, im-   |
                                        ↓
We feel that you are ideally suited to work with |
                                        ↓
I can answer your inquiry of March 12, 1972, when|
```

These lines came out almost to the outer limit or else exactly on it. You won't always be so lucky, of course.

Estimating What to Type in Ten Spaces

2. Suppose you have just typed the line ending with the word saw, and you are about to type the next word--when the bell rings:

After conferring with Mr. O.R. Jenkins, I saw __________ (Bell; ten spaces)

You have ten spaces. Here are some possible sets of words that could follow saw. Draw a short vertical line after the last letter you could type in each set before returning the carriage. You can follow the example. (You should also apply what you know about word division.)

EXAMPLE:

```
↓
a fine op|portunity to
```

```
    ↓                                 ↓
(a) that he would                 (f) unusual designs that I
    ↓                                 ↓
(b) a new approach that           (g) convenient solutions
    ↓                                 ↓
(c) something unusual             (h) why I won't be an
    ↓                                 ↓
(d) many different ways           (i) some of the reasons
    ↓                                 ↓
(e) things about the office       (j) who would probably
---------------------------
    ↓                                 ↓
(a) that he|would                 (f) unusual|designs that I
    ↓                                 ↓
(b) a new ap|proach that          (g) convenient|solutions
    ↓                                 ↓
(c) something|unusual             (h) why I|won't be an
    ↓                                 ↓
(d) many dif|ferent ways          (i) some of|the reasons
    ↓                                 ↓
(e) things|about the office       (j) who would|probably
```

3. Without counting, Estimate where you would end each line. Indicate this by drawing a vertical line just as you did in the previous exercise.

(a) Thank you for your letter of March 15. I was out of the office when

(b) I would like more information on the content before I make my decision

(c) The other members of the faculty objected to his suggestion. I found

(d) Whenever we play in Boston, the fans are so enthusiastic that we cannot

(e) On the other hand, few people in the United States are able to have this

(f) When they act, they usually do so with the children's interests in mind

(g) Students have a way of handling this kind of situation. In spring, for

(h) Whenever we try to take stock of ourselves, we find we are actually doing

(i) Perhaps you are wondering why we haven't used these methods. So far, we

(j) The only reason we haven't yet tried the new procedure is that it would

----

(a) Thank you for your letter of March 15. I was out of the of|fice when

(b) I would like more information on the content before I make|my decision

(c) The other members of the faculty objected to his suggestion.| I found

(d) Whenever we play in Boston, the fans are so enthusiastic that|we cannot

(e) On the other hand, few people in the United States are able|to have this

(f) When they act, they usually do so with the children's in|terests in mind

(g) Students have a way of handling this kind of situation. In|spring, for

(h) Whenever we try to take stock of ourselves, we find we are|actually doing

(i) Perhaps you are wondering why we haven't used these methods. |So far, we

(j) The only reason we haven't yet tried the new procedure is|that it would

After checking your sentences, you may want to try the Review of this section, on page 204. You should then consult the Chapter Guide to see which part of the book you want to study next.

CHAPTER EIGHT

Attending to Form

Whether you approve of Women's Lib or not, you'll agree that the girls have been a big help to letter writers.

A man is and always has been "Mr."--whether he has a wife or ever has had one. But before Women's Lib, a woman had to be careful how she signed her letters. If she dropped the "Mrs.," she was assumed to be "Miss." If she included the "Mrs.," she still had to keep people informed about her marital status by using the appropriate form of signature.

Women's Lib urges us to use the title "Ms." for any woman from six to sixty and beyond. And whether she's single, married, widowed, or divorced is her own business. (Perhaps Southerners always felt this way, since they have traditionally called a woman "Ms." Women's Lib merely formalized the title by giving it a proper spelling.)

Previous chapters in this book have been concerned with what we call the body of the letter--the part that actually carries the message. This chapter is about the other parts of letters and memos, including modern forms of address like "Ms." We can think of these parts as the Identification.

You may be surprised to learn that the forms presented here are not arbitrary rules that someone thought might look nice. We have adopted these forms because they really do give additional information to the reader. In particular, you will learn:

(a) how to identify the parts of the letter, letter styles, and punctuation styles; and
(b) how to word the different parts of the letter to prevent any confusion about their meaning.

Spacing suggestions are covered in the section FOR REFERENCE called Spacing Guide (page 239). They are also appropriate for the interoffice letter, or memo.

As usual, the preview to the chapter (page 205) will help you determine how you may best use the materials.

Figure 8-1

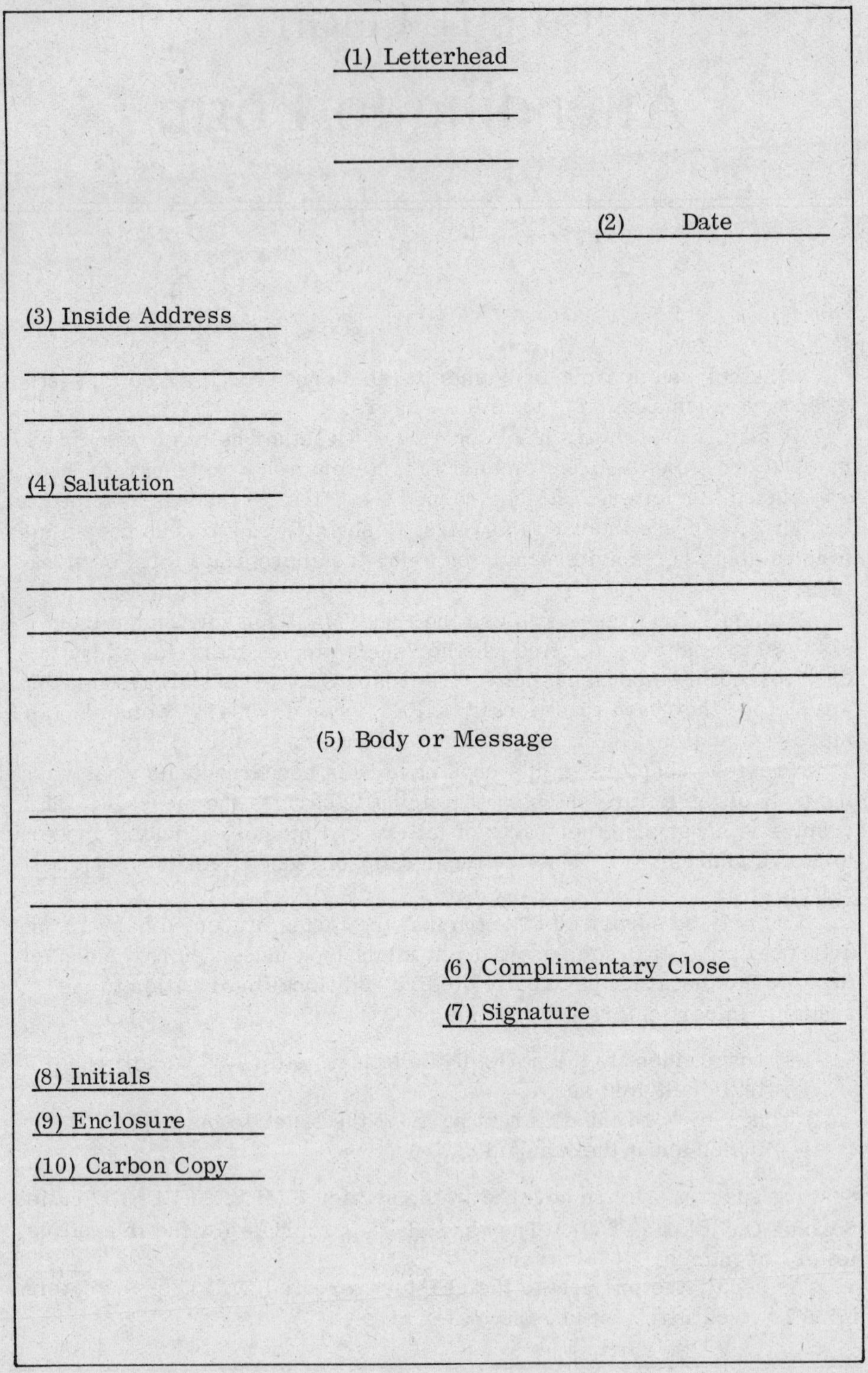

(1) Letterhead

(2) Date

(3) Inside Address

(4) Salutation

(5) Body or Message

(6) Complimentary Close

(7) Signature

(8) Initials

(9) Enclosure

(10) Carbon Copy

LETTER STYLES

1. Figure 8-1 shows the basic parts of the business letter. It also illustrates the most popular letter style, the block style. As you see, each paragraph begins flush with the left-hand margin, and so do most of the letter parts. This of course means that this style is easier to type than an indented style would be. The date, complimentary close, and the signature are as close to the right-hand margin as possible.

Familiarize yourself with these letter parts now. You don't need to memorize the names, however. They are given here only so we will have some common reference point.

2. There are two other popular letter styles: One is the semiblock style, which is exactly like the block style except that the first line in every paragraph is indented--usually five spaces, or sometimes as many as ten. The other letter style is full block style, in which every part of the letter starts flush with the left-hand margin. This style is getting more and more popular since it is the easiest style to type.

Another choice you have in your letters is in styling the punctuation. Closed punctuation is rarely used nowadays, because it's just too much trouble. In closed style, some sort of punctuation follows each line; a colon is placed after the date and a comma put after each line of the inside address. The most modern punctuation style is called open punctuation, in which no punctuation is used after any part of the letter.

The most popular style, however, is mixed punctuation, which is like open style except that it keeps the customary colon (or comma) after the salutation and a comma after the complimentary close.

Unless you work in an office that has its own standards, you may choose whatever punctuation style you prefer. Because it is most popular, mixed punctuation is used in the sample letters in this book. Semiblock paragraph style is used too, even if it isn't the most popular. The reason is that the sample letters here were double spaced for teaching purposes; and with double spacing, the indented paragraph style is easier to read, since the paragraphs are immediately apparent. (Most business letters are single spaced, however.)

Again, you don't need to remember the names of the letter styles or the punctuation styles--just the possibilities. From what you have just read, however, try to identify the various styles represented in the samples that follow.

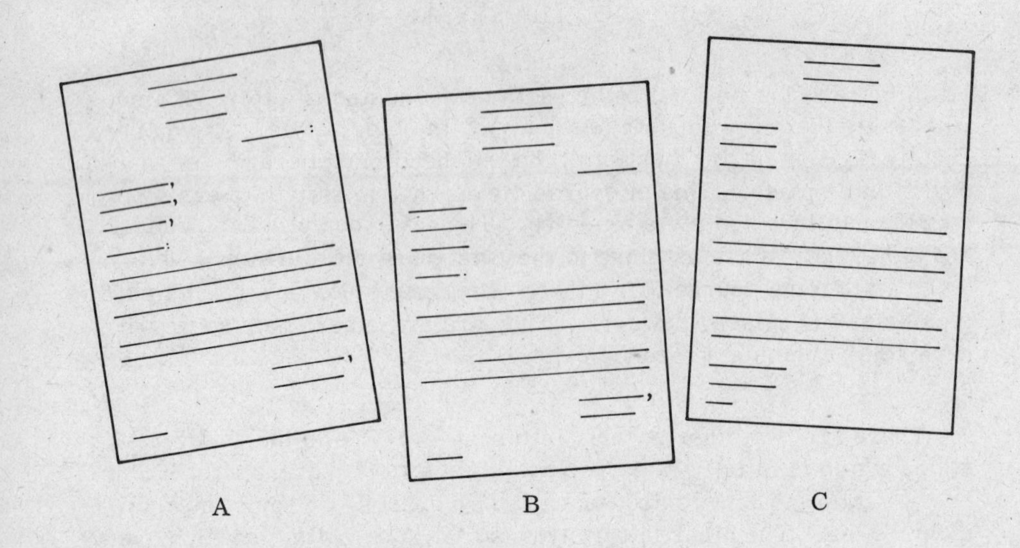

(a) Which is in semiblock style?_____
(b) Which is in block style?_____
(c) Which is in full-block style?_____
(d) Which is in open punctuation style?_____
(e) Which is in closed punctuation style?_____
(f) Which is in mixed punctuation style?_____
(g) If you wanted to pick a letter style and a punctuation style that would be easiest to type, which would you pick?_____

(a) B
(b) A
(c) C
(d) C
(e) A
(f) B
(g) full-block style and open punctuation style

LETTERHEAD AND DATE

3. Let's examine the parts of the letter in more detail. First, we will look at the letterhead and date, which are numbered (1) and (2) in Figure 8-1. As you'll see, we follow certain practices that will help the reader by adding information to the message.

(A)

The Bates Corporation
425 Connecticut Avenue, N.W.
Washington, D.C. 20008

LO-4-5677

January 5, 1972

Dear Mr. Jones:

But on a home job, with just blank stationery, the address and the date go together. This homemade variety is called the return address. As Sample B shows, the return address consists of a street line; a city, state, and zip code line; and a date line.

(B)

35 Bergen Avenue
Hartford, Conn. 10021
January 6, 1972

Dear Mr. Jones:

If you look over both samples, you will notice that we use only two abbreviations in the address: One is for a direction ("N.W." for "Northwest"); the other is the abbreviation for the state or "D.C." for "District of Columbia." You may spell out the name of the state, if you prefer. You also have a choice between the new, simplified abbreviations for states and the longer abbreviations you learned in grammar school. Table 1 on page 229 lists the state abbreviations in both styles.*

Something else to notice is that each sample prepares the reader for the letter that will follow. For example, the letterhead of Sample A notifies the reader that the letter is from an individual who represents a business. And the return address of Sample B points out that the letter is from an individual representing himself.

What other information does the reader get from Sample A that he doesn't get from Sample B? ______________________________

- - - - - - - - - - - - - -

Sample A also supplies the phone number.

*Although you may choose either abbreviation for the name of the state when you write an inside address, you probably should start getting accustomed to using the new form on envelopes since the postal service can pick up this style with its scanners. This should mean faster mail deliveries.

INSIDE ADDRESS

4. The inside address, number (3) in Figure 8-1, comes after the letterhead and date. This is always flush with the left-hand margin, regardless of the letter style; and it consists of the reader's name and address. Usually the first line is the reader's name. Next comes the company's name, which should be exactly the same as it appears in the company's letterhead--same spellings and same abbreviations. The address is last.

A title is always given with the name, and most often precedes it. If the person has a special title, like "Professor" or "Dr.," we use this. (Table 2 on page 230 lists the correct forms for special titles.) If the person doesn't have a special title, we simply address him or her as "Mr." or "Ms." Here are a few examples:

(A)	(B)	(C)
Dr. Corrinne Smathers	Mr. Perry Bryce	Ms. Joan Perry

Of course, when using "Ms." you'll have to size up your reader first. If you're writing to a "Mrs." who says she worked hard to earn her "M-R-S" degree, then by all means call her "Mrs." Also continue to address an elderly, single, conservative woman as "Miss." Still, "Ms." makes good sense, and we all should start using it. Nowadays, many employment offices will ask a new employee what she prefers to be called, and many female employees choose "Ms."

You may also address a professional man or woman by using an academic degree following the name; it is set off from the name with a comma, as here:

(D)	(E)
Corrinne Smathers, M.D.	Corrinne Smathers, Ph.D.

Of course, you would never write "Dr. Corrinne Smathers, M.D.," or "Dr. Corrinne Smathers, Ph.D." This would be giving the same information twice. Nor would you address anyone by using "B.A." or "B.S.," since these are only first-level college degrees.

Sometimes you might want to give a business or professional title. This goes after the name, as here:

(F)

Dr. Corrinne Smathers, Chairman
English Department
Columbia University
New York, New York 10026

As you see, this business or professional title is capitalized and set off from the last name by a comma. If this title is long (at least two or more words), it belongs on the next line for balance.

Suppose you were writing a letter to Diana Bland--a young woman with no academic title. Her business or professional title, however, is "Technical Advisor" to Newark Educational Corporation, 245 Schley St., Newark, New Jersey 10025. Write the correct inside address:

Ms. Diana Bland OR Miss Diana Bland
Technical Advisor
Newark Educational Corporation
245 Schley Street
Newark, New Jersey 10025

(Did you remember to either spell out New Jersey or to use a correct abbreviation?)

5. There is something else you should remember about the street name. In large cities, where most business letters are written and received, many of the street names are numbers. (We discussed this in Chapter 7.) These can easily be confused with the house numbers. For this reason, the following practices were adopted:

IF THE STREET NAME IS	THEN	EXAMPLE
(a) "First" through "Tenth,"	(a) spell it out.	(a) 345 First Avenue
(b) a number higher than "Tenth," but set off from the house number by a direction like "East,"	(b) use the figure.	(b) 3 West 43 Street
(c) a number higher than "Tenth," but not set off from the house number by a direction like East.	(c) use the figure plus st., rd., or th--whichever is appropriate.	(c) 3 43rd Street

Try copyediting each of the following return addresses so they follow all the standards. You may delete any unnecessary punctuation, add any punctuation that is missing, or do whatever is needed.

(a) 11 11 St.
N.Y. N.Y. , 10001
Feb. 4 1970

(b) 424 Wisc. Ave. NE
Wash. D.C. 20007
Mar. 17 1972

(c) 11 E. 10 St.
N. Haven Conn., 52104
August 3 1972

(d) 423 S. Barrington Rd.
N. Barrington Mass. 50900
Oct. 4th 1972

(a) 11 11th Street
New York, N.Y. 10001
February 4, 1970

(b) 424 Wisconsin Ave., N.E.
Washington, D.C. 20007
March 17, 1972

(c) 11 East Tenth Street
New Haven, Conn. 52104
August 3, 1972

(d) 423 South Barrington Road
North Barrington, Mass. 50900
October 4, 1972

SALUTATION AND ATTENTION

6. Number (4) in Figure 8-1 is the salutation, or the greeting. You should make sure that the name and title are exactly the same as they are in the inside address. But the other wording depends on the tone you want to set. Here are some examples.

TONE	SALUTATION
Informal and personal	Dear John, OR Dear Kathy:
Usual	Dear Mr. Green: OR Dear Ms. Green:
Formal and personal	My dear Mr. Jones: OR My dear Mrs. Jones:
Very formal	Sir: OR Madam:

As you probably know already, the first word of the salutation is always capitalized; and so are any other nouns or titles. Notice that a comma may follow the informal and personal greeting.

The correct salutation for a letter to an organization is "Gentlemen" plus a colon, and not "Dear Sir." Sometimes you may want to direct the letter to the attention of a special person in the organization. In that case, you may use what is called an attention line. Most people put it below the inside address, and flush left or centered--as you like it. But sometimes it also appears in the second line of the inside address. Here are two possible styles to use:

ATTENTION DISTRICT FORCE MANAGER

Attention Ms. Margolies

Occasionally a salutation is directed to more than one person. In that case, the first names are dropped--but not the titles. Assume you were writing to two ladies, a Ms. Rozanna Brown and a Ms. Jo Kelly.

(a) How would you address them?______________________________
(b) How would you address their husbands (Pete Brown and Frank Kelly) if you were writing one letter addressed to them both?

____

- - - - - - - - - - - - - -

(a) Dear Ms. Brown and Ms. Kelly:
(b) Dear Mr. Brown and Mr. Kelly:

SUBJECT LINE

7. Occasionally--and particularly in a memo--you may want to key the reader to your topic. If so, you use a subject line, which goes below the salutation. Like the attention line, it may be either flush left or centered. There are also several possible styles. Look at these, for example:

ADVANTAGES OF NO-FAULT INSURANCE

Advantages of No-Fault Insurance

SUBJECT: ADVANTAGES OF NO-FAULT INSURANCE

In re: Advantages of No-Fault Insurance

Re: Advantages of No-Fault Insurance

After the subject line, if there is one, comes the body of the letter. This is number (5) in Figure 8-1. With these parts in mind, we are now ready for review.

Read the situation first, and then write an inside address and salutation. Include an attention line, if it's needed.

SITUATION (a): The letter is to a woman named Claire Rose. She is Personnel Manager of Macy's, 2 Herald Sq., NYC 10011. Give the usual salutation.

SITUATION (b): The letter is to Bloomingdale's, but to the attention of the Personnel Manager. The store is at 58 E. 59 St., New York City, 10016.

(a) Ms. Claire Rose
Macy's
2 Herald Square
New York, New York 10011

Dear Ms. Rose:

(b) Bloomingdale's
58 East 59 Street
New York, New York 10016
ATTENTION: PERSONNEL MANAGER

Gentlemen:

COMPLIMENTARY CLOSE

8. Let's look now at the complimentary close, number (6) in Figure 8-1. As with the salutation, the exact wording to use depends on the tone you want. Look at the samples on the following page.

TONE	CLOSE
Personal	Sincerely, Warmly, Cordially, Cordially yours, Sincerely yours,
More formal	Yours truly, Yours very truly, Very truly yours, Respectfully yours, Very cordially yours, Very sincerely yours,

As you see, the close is followed by a comma, and only the first word of the expression is capitalized.

You may also use a standard but informal close like "Best wishes." Or you might want to be more inventive, as this letter writer was:

> Dear John:
>
> Thanks for the booklet Motivation. I'm previewing some of the films it suggested.
>
> Yours for a more motivated world.
>
> Geary Rummler, Ph.D.

Remember, you set the tone you want.

This time, suggest a possible salutation to John Carter for each of these closes:

(a) ____________________ (b) ____________________

Cordially, Very sincerely yours,

- - - - - - - - - - - - - -

(a) Dear John: OR Dear John,
(b) Dear Mr. Carter: OR My dear Mr. Carter:

SIGNATURE

9. The signature--number (8) in Figure 8-1--is usually directly below the close. It may include a company signature as well as a writer's signature to emphasize that the company shares the writer's view. Either of two forms is possible.

As Sample A shows, the company signature may follow the complimentary close. A space comes next (for the writer's pen-and-ink signature) and then the writer's name and professional or business title.

Sample B is equally acceptable. Here the space for the writer's pen-and-ink signature follows the close. Then comes the company name, and next is the writer's name and title.

(A)
Sincerely yours,
The Bates Company
Clarence Dander
Clarence Dander, Manager

(B)
Sincerely yours,
Clarence Dander
The Bates Company
Clarence Dander, Manager

The "Mr." is never used (although rock star Alice Cooper might use it to prevent us from confusing him with a female). A "Miss" isn't used either, nor is a "Ms." However, a married woman who doesn't want to be addressed as "Miss" or "Ms." should type her signature as follows:

IF SHE IS	HER SIGNATURE IS	EXAMPLE
(a) living with her husband or widowed,	(a) Mrs. + first name + last name	(a) Mrs. Jean Rich OR Mrs. Paul Rich
(b) divorced,	(b) Mrs. + maiden name + last name OR Mrs. + first name + maiden name + last name	(b) Mrs. Miller Rich OR Mrs. Jean Miller Rich

Remember that a professional man or woman may want to use an academic degree. This follows the name and is set off from it by a comma, as here:

(C)
Clement Chan, Ph.D.

As you probably know, the pen-and-ink signature should never have a title. Give your full name to be formal; but give just your first name to a friend. You may also give just your first name to a business acquaintance if you are on a first-name basis.

If you are signing for your employer, you should follow his name by a slash plus your initials, like this:

(D)
Sincerely yours,
Eileen Hogan/mp
Eileen Hogan

Now the reader knows that Eileen Hogan is responsible for the words and that "mp" merely signed the letter in Ms. Hogan's absence.

Write a close, a typed signature form, and a pen-and-ink signature for the following:

(a) Dear Clark,

____

(From his good friend Miss Marjorie Wrye)

(b) Dear Mr. Calloway

____

(From Mr. Paul Stone, who is the personnel director of Bloomingdale's.)

(a) Warmly,
Marjorie
Marjorie Wrye

(b) Yours truly,
Bloomingdale's
Paul Stone
Paul Stone
Personnel Director
OR
Yours truly,
Paul Stone
Bloomingdale's
Paul Stone
Personnel Director

INITIALS, ENCLOSURES, CARBON COPIES

10. Last is the information at the bottom of the letter--numbers (8), (9), and (10) in Figure 8-1. The initials are the writer's initials and also those of the typist. They help the reader if he should have a question. Maybe an enclosure was promised but not sent. He may phone and ask the typist about it rather than the president of the company. The initials

can also be of help to a writer who uses a typing pool. They are also a reference, in the company's file, to who wrote the letter and who typed it.

There are various styles for the initials. But the following are most popular:

(A)		(B)
MBG/ee	OR	MBG:ec

As you see, the writer's initials are capital letters and the typist's are small ones, to show who has the major responsibility.

An enclosure is used if something is to be included in the envelope. This notifies the reader to be on the lookout, and not to toss it into the wastebasket accidentally. If there is only one enclosure, the word Enclosure is enough; with more than one item, use Enclosures. The items may be listed by name, or you can give just the total. As an example:

(C)	(D)
Enclosures 1. Check 2. Deposit Slip	Enclosures 2

Last is carbon copies. Copies of the letter are often sent to other persons. If so, you must notify the reader by using "CC" or "cc" for "carbon copy." This notation follows the enclosure. Again, any of several styles is good. Here are some possibilities:

(E)	(F)	(G)
cc Ms. Coffee Mr. Tea	CC: Mr. Coffee Ms. Tea	cc: Mrs. L. Coffee Mr. Tea

Probably the most popular style is example G.

These are all the parts of a letter, except for an occasional postscript at the end, which, as you probably know, begins with a "P.S." Remember, though, a postscript isn't used very often in business letters, because it suggests an afterthought. However, when it's there, you follow the same paragraphing forms you used throughout the letter.

Suppose you were writing a business letter at home. You had already typed your signature and signed it in pen and ink, as follows. Write this sentence as a postscript: The meeting is at 8:00 sharp!

Cordially,
Tom
Tom Frost

P.S. The meeting is at 8:00 sharp!

SETTING UP A LETTER

11. Try setting up the following letter. If you prefer, you may do this on the typewriter. In that case you would want to follow the correct spacing. Check the Spacing Guide in FOR REFERENCE, on page 239. Let's assume that this letter is of average length.

> SITUATION: The date is January 3, 1972. The letter is from Larry Putnam, of 33 W. 8th St., N.Y.C., 10011, to the circulation manager of The New Yorker, 25 W. 43rd St., 10017, on the subject of new subscriptions. Mr. Putnam typed the letter himself, and he's sending a copy of his bill with it.

----

33 West Eighth Street
New York, New York 10011
January 3, 1972

The New Yorker
25 West 43 Street
New York, New York 10017

ATTENTION CIRCULATION MANAGER

Gentlemen:

SUBJECT: NEW SUBSCRIPTIONS

Yours very truly,
Larry Putnam
Larry Putnam

12. Now set up this letter. Again, follow the guidelines for spacing given in the Spacing Guide (page 239).

SITUATION: The letter was written on January 26, 1972, and is from Berta Fields, who is art director for John Wiley & Sons, Inc., 603 3rd Ave., NYC, 10021. She is writing to Ben Cohen, a professor at N. York University, Washington Sq., NYC, 10011. Berta prefers all modern forms of address whenever possible. She doesn't know the professor. She is sending a copy of this letter to another professor, Arthur James; and her secretary, Elsie White, typed it for her.

Check your setup with the suggestion. You may then do the Review of Chapter 8 on page 207, if you would like to check on your progress. Then consult the Chapter Guide to see where to go from here.

John Wiley & Sons, Inc.
603 Third Avenue
New York, New York 10021
January 26, 1972

Professor Ben Cohen
New York University
Washington Square
New York, New York 10011

Dear Professor Cohen:

Very sincerely yours,
Berta Fields
John Wiley & Sons, Inc.
Berta Fields
Art Director

BF: ew
cc: Professor Arthur James

OR

Very sincerely yours,
John Wiley & Sons, Inc.
Berta Fields
Berta Fields
Art Director

CHAPTER NINE
Writing Your Resume

Personnel directors tell stories of the careless job applicants who write "None," or "Only once" beside the question "Sex" on the employment application. More sophisticated job seekers may laugh, but they too often supply information that is irrelevant. They tell personal things no prospective employer would dare to ask--or should even care to know. More important, they don't tell a prospective employer what he does want to know: what they have done that would make them valuable commodities.

In this chapter you will learn how to write a summary of your accomplishments. We call this summary a resume, from the French. It should include everything a prospective employer wants to know about you and nothing more. The overriding principle to keep in mind is that someone in business is primarily interested in making a profit, which means that his only real interest in you is how you can help him do this. In writing your resume, then, you must put yourself in his place: What would he want to know about you?

There are already too many rules about writing resumes, many of them conflicting. As a result, most people are confused about what to include and what not to include. And some people are so confused that they remain in jobs they no longer enjoy.

What such people need is a fresh start. For this reason, there is no preview. Study this chapter if you want some step-by-step help in writing a resume.

FOCUS ON ONE OBJECTIVE

1. Before we consider the actual writing of a resume, let's talk about approaching it with the right frame of mind.

Always remember that the purpose of writing a resume is to help you get a job. A resume may not be your right arm, but it is certainly your best foot. And you had better put it forward. The way to do this is to focus on one kind of job--maybe even on one particular job you know is available.

The same advice applies even if you have many skills and many talents that you want to display. A surplus of talents and skills is always a plus, because it means that you have many more opportunities for suitable jobs. Do you like to teach, and to write, and to manage people? And have you had experience in each of these areas? Then you're lucky, because you could get any one of three totally different kinds of job. Take your pick. If you like, you may apply for all three jobs, using a different resume for each. But you would focus on your teaching accomplishments in your resume for a teaching job; on your writing accomplishments in your resume for a writing job; and on your managerial accomplishments in your resume for a management job.

The wise practice is to write one resume for each job category--and maybe even for each particular job.

Unfortunately, most people don't have a clear objective before they write their resumes. What happens then is that they tell everything, whether it is relevant or not. As an example, look at the beginning of a resume written by Marianne Reilly. Considering that the prospective employer would get this information about Marianne before he knows anything else about her, would you say offhand that she has put her best foot forward?

NAME: Marianne Reilly | APPEARANCE: Attractive
AGE: 22 | HEALTH: Excellent
WEIGHT: 122 pounds | HOBBY: Dancing
HEIGHT: 5'6" | SCHOOL: St. Regis High School Library, Pennsylvania

The answer to the question is: It depends. If Marianne is applying for a job as a Playboy Bunny, or for the title "Miss Subways," her resume starts out just fine. But if she wants to be someone's secretary, she may be asking for trouble. If she hopes to be an engineering aide, she is either asking for trouble or wasting her time--depending on the engineer.

Suppose Marianne Reilly has some excellent secretarial skills in addition to her obvious physical assets. She hears of two jobs that she would be interested in. One is a job as a hostess in a good supper club. The other is a job as a secretary to a lawyer in a small law firm.

Ordinarily, a resume might not be required for either of these jobs. However, let's say that Marianne is out of town and has no choice but to send a resume to each prospective employer.

(a) Which of her assets should she stress in the resume directed to the owner of the supper club?
(b) Which of her assets should she stress in her resume directed to the lawyer?

- - - - - - - - - - - - - - -

(a) She should stress her physical assets in the resume for the owner of the supper club.
(b) She should stress her secretarial skills in her resume for the lawyer.

ASSETS AND LIABILITIES

2. Don't worry if your qualifications fail to measure up to all the demands of your prospective employers. Perhaps, nobody's qualifications could. Just take stock of yourself honestly, so you can stress your assets and play down your liabilities.

Most people are wise enough to play down a job failure and to be prepared to explain it. Failure on a job is a human condition, and may even be necessary, since we human beings learn from our mistakes.

However, you should not confuse any attempt to explain or deemphasize a job failure or a missing skill with any attempt to falsify your credentials. To say you are a college graduate when you've had just a few college courses is a criminal offense called fraud. A few years ago, in a sensational case, a New York welfare director used false degrees from false colleges as stepping stones to some embarrassingly high places. Eventually she was caught, and she is probably languishing in some embarrassingly low jail.

Fraud doesn't happen very often, fortunately. What does happen--and very often--is that people defraud themselves by failing to stress their assets. Or they fail to look for any special circumstances that might compensate for what they feel is a liability.

Let's examine the following situation to see which experiences are assets and which are liabilities for Mary G., if she wants a technical job.

> SITUATION: Mary G. is a housewife in her early forties who hasn't worked in fifteen years. She is a graduate of Wellesley College, and she has a B.S. in chemistry. Before retiring to be a housewife and mother, she had a job as a laboratory assistant at Hoffman La Roche, a drug company in New Jersey. Last year, in preparation for returning to work, she took a course in computer programming at Rutgers University. She did quite well.

You would probably agree that Mary's liability is her lack of recent experience. So, instead of stressing job experience in her resume,

Mary G. should stress her excellent technical education. This isn't being dishonest--it is just putting her best foot forward.

But suppose Mary G. decided she wanted a job as a house mother for a college fraternity. What would she emphasize in her resume now? Would she have to play anything down?

- - - - - - - - - - - - - - - -

Now Mary would emphasize her education and her experience as a housewife and mother. She doesn't have to play anything down for this job; she has nothing to hide.

3. Try assessing each of these situations from the standpoint of assets and liabilities for a particular job.

> SITUATION (a): Ken J. has been educated at Exeter, and he has a B.A. in English from Yale. He is in his early thirties. His experience has been both as a teacher of English in a high school and as a technical writer in a large corporation. Now he is writing his resume for a job as an editor with a science publisher.

(1) What should he stress?______________________________

(2) What will he have to play down?______________________________

> SITUATION (b): Bart D. is a recent graduate of a good business school--Pace College. He has had experience in a great number of semiskilled jobs. However, he had those jobs while he was going to school and therefore didn't hold any of them very long. He gets along extremely well with people. Now he is writing his resume for a job as a personnel interviewer with a large corporation.

(1) What should he stress?______________________________

(2) What will he have to play down?______________________________

- - - - - - - - - - - - - - - -

(a-1) He should stress his writing and language skills; he should also stress his ability to work well in a technical field even though technical subjects were not his specialty in school.
(a-2) He should play down his small experience in publishing.
(b-1) He should stress his experience in many different jobs and his ability to get along with people.
(b-2) He should play down his short stays in each job and explain that he had to fit these jobs in with his school schedule.

GENERAL PATTERN

4. Now we shall turn to the actual writing of the resume. It helps to approach this just as you would approach any other kind of business communication. The first thing to look for is a general pattern that you will be able to follow. Fortunately, a resume has one, as Figure 9-1 illustrates.

Did you notice that the general pattern of a resume is like that of a Telling letter? First is the Identification, which consists of the applicant's name, address, and phone number. Next is the Orientation, which is the applicant's job objective--the kind of job he wants.

The third portion of the resume consists of the Information. As you see in Figure 9-1, the major employment is first, beginning with the present job and continuing backwards to the first major job. Our sample applicant G.I. Joe was young and had just one major job besides his military service. Next comes any miscellaneous employment the applicant has had, like part-time or relatively minor jobs. Then comes the applicant's education. Since Mr. Joe had only two years of college and no degree, he listed his high school too. However, a college graduate who has been out of school for a long time probably wouldn't do this.

The last portion of the resume is the Addition. This includes any personal data the applicant wants to include--and he doesn't have to tell anything he doesn't feel would help him. In Mr. G.I. Joe's case, he obviously felt that marriage and children are assets. Note that references are mentioned only as being available. Overall, a good resume is short, simple, and sincere.

From what you see in Figure 9-1 and also from what has been said here so far, what would you say is the key to the resume?

The Information is the key.

IDENTIFICATION AND ORIENTATION

5. Let's consider the parts of the resume, starting with the Identification and the Orientation.

The Orientation, or job objective, is your focus. And, as you would expect, the decision about it is the hard part--in other words, deciding what to focus on among all possible jobs and careers one might have. The actual writing of the job objective is simple indeed, since it is just a statement of what you want to do. But it must be actually stated and not just "kept in mind"--both for the sake of the prospective employer,

Figure 9-1

[Identification] Resume of G.I. Joe

120 Tyler St.
Pittsfield, Mass. 91201
442-4567

[Orientation]

JOB OBJECTIVE
Assistant manager of a retail store

INFORMATION

EMPLOYMENT

January 1971- January 1973	England Brothers, Pittsfield, Mass. General Department Store Assistant buyer in men's wear
	I introduced a new line of men's shirts which was reordered three times during the first season and increased sales by $10,000.
	I supervised a salesforce of 7 men and women, and 2 floor managers. I also introduced a policy of hiring part-time workers.
	I maintained a standard inventory and did all the ordering myself.

MILITARY SERVICE

November 1969- November 1971	I was a quartermaster sergeant assisting the captain in charge of PX operations at Fort Dix, N.J.

MISCELLANEOUS EMPLOYMENT

September 1963- June 1967	I had part-time selling jobs while going to school, and also for 6 months before going into the service.

EDUCATION

	Regional High School, Dalton, Mass.
September 1967- June 1969	Pittsfield Community College, Pittsfield, Mass. A 2-year merchandising course
January 1971- July 1971	England Brothers Buyers Course

[Addition]

PERSONAL
I am married, and have two children.

REFERENCES
These are available.

who will learn what you want to do, and for your own sake as well. The job objective is the target. And everything you say later, either in the resume itself or in the job interview, will be viewed through it.

If you are writing the resume for a particular job, it is obvious how to phrase the job objective. As an example, Mitchell Keyes wrote a resume to apply for the job of principal of Clearwater High School. His job objective was as follows:

> JOB OBJECTIVE
>
> I would like to be the principal of Clearwater High School.

Or he might have started with the word Principal.

On the other hand, Jack Balkan wanted to be a principal of a high school too. But he didn't have a particular job to apply for. This is his job objective:

> JOB OBJECTIVE
>
> I would like to be the principal of a medium-sized, rural high school.

(Again, he might have started with the word Principal.) He also might have been willing to take a job in a large school or a city school or both. Writing the job objective gives the applicant the chance to be as specific as he likes.

Now write the Identification and Orientation for Olive Pitts, of Main Dalton Road, Windsor, Massachusetts 069095. Her phone is 684-3260. She wants to be an administrative assistant to an executive in a large corporation.

Resume of Olive Pitts	Main Dalton Road Windsor, Massachusetts 06095 Phone: 684-3260

JOB OBJECTIVE

I would like to be an administrative assistant to an executive in a large corporation.

OR

Administrative assistant to an executive in a large corporation.

(Whether you choose the sentence form or just the phrase is not important; you may choose whichever form "sounds" better to you.)

INFORMATION

6. Next, but most important, is the Information. Before you write this part, you'll have to make several decisions. Your first decision is how to organize it. As you saw in Figure 9-1, the general pattern of the Information is employment first, miscellaneous employment next, and education last. However, like all the patterns you have used in this book, the pattern for the key part of the resume--the Information--is flexible.

Suppose you are a new graduate, and you have never had a regular job. You obviously wouldn't start with major employment or even miscellaneous employment. You should then start with your education, and particularly if you have had good training or were successful in school. You would give your college major and your minor and any special achievements.

On the other hand, suppose you had only one full-time job but very prestigious and relevant miscellaneous experience. In that case you might want to give all of your job experience under the heading of "Employment," and indicate (in parentheses and under the date) what was full-time employment and what was part-time.

Or maybe you have had only one job, say in government or in a large organization like the telephone company, and you were in that job for about ten or fifteen years. You might then want to treat job promotions as if they had been separate jobs with different companies.

Maybe you have job-hopped a bit, or you haven't worked steadily for one reason or another. In that case, you might not want to give a chronological accounting of your time, but you might want to organize your resume by job function instead. (You could of course account for your time year by year, if asked. Chances are you wouldn't be asked, however.) For example, if you have worked both as a writer and as an editor for a number of years, you might want to list your accomplishments under two headings: Writing Assignments and Editing Assignments.

Suppose you have worked as a freelance illustrator for most of your working career, and you have had many different assignments.

How would you organize your resume: by function or by a yearly history?______________________________

- - - - - - - - - - - - - -

You would organize by function. (Your major headings might be: Work for Large Companies and Work for Individuals.)

7. Once you have decided how to organize the Information, your next decision is what the content will be. And for this you must refer to your job objective.

Make a list, on a separate sheet of paper, of the four or five major job accomplishments of a person who already has a job like the one you want. We can define a job accomplishment here as what a person actually gets done after some reasonable period of time has elapsed.

Although these job accomplishments will not actually appear in your resume, they are vital because you will need to relate your own work and educational experience to them. You will be able to do this easily if you're applying for the same kind of work you have done before. But you should do this even if you are applying for a totally new kind of job to see if you have had any similar experiences. (Of course, it goes without saying that if you have never done the work before, and you have not had the appropriate education, it is probably not the job for you.)

Let's take a teaching job as an example, since we all know what teachers do in general, even if we haven't been teachers ourselves. The major accomplishments of a high school Spanish teacher at the end of a semester might be as follows:

(a) I taught twenty-five students how to use the present tense in Spanish; I also taught them how to say, read, and write simple Spanish sentences.
(b) I evaluated this group.
(c) I supervised a Spanish Club.
(d) I monitored the study hall once a day.
(e) I was teachers' representative at the PTA meetings.

So, she taught a subject matter; she tested her group; she supervised another group; she monitored still another group; and she represented still one more group.

Even if you haven't been a teacher yourself, you may have done something that you can somehow relate to each of these job accomplishments. (You must also be fluent in Spanish, of course.) The purpose of showing these relationships is to show the prospective employer that you can do the work.

Let's take another job everyone knows about--that of a women's shoes salesman in a large department store. See if you can write four or five job accomplishments for him--things he gets done in a day that help the store make a profit. (You can invent details like the number of people he waited on.)

(a) I selected styles that were suitable for about twenty-five different women.
(b) I measured and fit these women with suitable shoes.
(c) I wrote up sales checks.
(d) I tallied my sales book and checked out the register at the end of the day.
(e) I brought out and returned to stock about fifty pairs of shoes.

8. You may need to do some research to be sure you have listed all the important job accomplishments of a person who holds a job like the one you want. But this research should bring you a handsome return, since the more specific you can be here, the better you will be able to show that you can do the job too (without saying so).

Remember, you're going to describe your own job with as many general job accomplishments as possible. Your own job descriptions will be slightly longer--maybe three lines or four. Each description must be related to one job accomplishment, and, if possible, tell what you have done like it. When you are ready, you should type up your resume with the job descriptions single spaced, but with a line between each description as a help to the reader.

Don't be modest. Start with "I" or with the past tense of a strong action verb: "I directed," or "Organized," or "Saved." You're going to concentrate on specific things you have done. You don't need to praise yourself in general terms, since your deeds will speak for themselves.

But you may take credit for a product that you produced even if you had some assistants, provided you would have been responsible had the project failed.

Let's take an example. Assume that Fred L. is applying for a job as a supervisor of a training department in a large corporation. He knows that the former supervisor had the following accomplishments after a year on the job:

(a) He supervised a staff of twenty-five in the production of fifteen books.
(b) He edited these materials for their technical accuracy.
(c) He supervised the production (typing, drafting) stages.
(d) He wrote proposals to the Government suggesting new projects.
(e) He wrote monthly progress reports to his company.

These job accomplishments will not appear on Fred's resume. But they are the raw materials he will use in describing his own accomplishments.

Actually, Fred is trying to move up from a position in a smaller company to the same position in a larger company. In his last job, which he held from October 1968 to January 1973, he directed the preparation of ten courses, with a staff of ten men and women assisting him. He also directed the testing. Fred not only edited the materials for their technical accuracy, but he copyedited them and carried them through the production stage. He was also extremely well liked by all of those who worked with him.

Here's how Fred might have written two of his job descriptions:

	EMPLOYMENT
October 1968 to January 1973	I.T. Title, 32 Mass. Avenue, Boston An accounting firm Director of Training Department I supervised a staff of 10 men and women in all stages of the writing of 10 training courses for accountants. I edited these materials for their technical accuracy as well as for their style.

See if you can write a third job description and relate it to the job accomplishment of supervising the production staff. Also bring in (without saying so) Fred's ability to work with people by mentioning that the production staff once volunteered to work overtime for Fred at no extra fee in order to meet a rough deadline.

I supervised the production staff. In doing so, I found all the people extremely cooperative. On one occasion, they volunteered to work overtime at no extra pay in order for us to meet a tight deadline.

ADDITION

9. You won't be able to relate everything you have done to an accomplishment for a job you're trying to win. But keep this as a goal anyway, as you write your job descriptions. Also, you wouldn't need to be so detailed about a job you held ten years ago as you would about your most recent job.

Now, at last, you're down to the last part of the resume: the personal and the references. About the personal, keep in mind that the purpose of the resume is to get a potential employer interested in how you can increase his profits. He really doesn't care about your personal life until he's sure he wants you. He can ask you what he wants to know about your family, or anything else, when he interviews you.

Nowadays, the Equal Employment Opportunity Commission (EEOC) cooperates nicely in allowing job applicants to keep their private lives private. Employers may no longer ask such basics as your age, your sex, your race, your color, or your religion. So if you suspect any of these would be liabilities, or if you just don't care to disclose them to a prospective employer, don't include a personal section in your resume at all.

Sometimes these small rebellions backfire, however. A year or so ago, a young woman named Thorne decided not to give her sex on the application form to a national testing service that was to process her application to law schools. She felt that these schools might discriminate against women applicants. Unfortunately, her applications were never processed, because the testing service put its faith in a computer. The computer chased her through as a male and found no record of her. (It wasn't smart enough to guess she might be a female.)

Today, Thorne might want the law schools to know she is a qualified female applicant. Qualified females are moving up in all fields. So are qualified blacks and Orientals and everyone else who has ever been treated unfairly before. Women's Lib is having its effect, and so is the EEOC.

Something else you don't have to state on your resume is your salary requirement. All salary details can wait until the employer is anxious to hire you. He might just offer you more than you would have dared to ask for initially.

So much for personal, and now let's talk about references. The rule is, never list them on your resume. You don't want anyone bothering your references until you are fairly sure you and the prospective employer are going to come to some agreement. References who are asked too often can get so tired of the job that they become less enthusiastic about the applicant. All you need to say on your resume is that you will supply references, or that references are available.

(a) From what we have said here, can you think of any reason for not sending a photograph? (Many times you are asked to do this when you apply for a job by mail.)

(b) Can you think of any circumstances that might make you want to send a photograph?

(a) You would not send a photograph if you wanted to conceal your physical appearance from your prospective employer until you have met him in an interview.
(b) You might have some physical assets that you want to display without specifically mentioning them in your resume. Maybe you are a young, beautiful black girl, for example, and you have a suspicion that your employer would like to hire blacks. The photograph will speak for you.

USING YOUR RESUME

10. How should you use your resume? This question has more answers than there are rules about resumes. Some experts say to write a resume and to send it to prospective employers with a cover letter. Other experts say by all means not to do this. Charles Boll is one. In his book Executive Jobs Limited, published by Macmillan Company, Mr. Boll is adament: Never send your resume by mail when you want an executive position. He advised that you send instead what he calls a "broadcast" letter directly to the presidents of firms you might be interested in working for. The purpose of such letters is to interest prospective employers in interviewing you. If you are applying for an executive position, you should at least read Mr. Boll's advice.

There are certainly times when you must send your resume with a cover letter, despite anyone's advice. Maybe you are several hundreds of miles away; you would be willing to relocate; but you wouldn't be willing to finance--or even make--a long trip to see about a job before knowing that the prospective employer might be interested in you. Why not send the resume then? There are many other circumstances too, when sending a resume looks like the sensible thing to do. In this matter, as in everything else, you must be guided by what seems best for you.

As a final exercise in this book, see if you can write your own resume following the suggestions given in this chapter. You may use Figure 9-1 as a guide for the form. If you are still in school, you can show how some of your courses are related to the accomplishments of the job you have chosen. But whether you are still in school or actually on the job, focus your job descriptions in your resume on what you have done rather than on how great you are. Remember, your deeds need no praise from you. Let your prospective employers do this for you. If you would like to see some resumes first, turn to page 219 in FOR REFERENCE and study the samples there.

RESUME

Closing Remarks

Chapter 9, Writing Your Resume, concludes Communicating By Letter. It seems like a sensible way to conclude, since writing a resume sums up all the skills you have learned in the other chapters.

The rest of the book is just what it says: FOR REFERENCE. There are form letters to use when you don't find it economical to spend time composing your own letters. You can then use the substance of a form letter and merely substitute your own details.

There are also blank outline forms for the business people who prefer to write their own letters. They may also find these outlines useful when they dictate to their secretaries.

Several tables are included that you will find helpful. One of these, Glossary of Selected Business Terms, is especially useful when you write on technical matters that are outside your field. A few sample resumes are presented, too, to give you hints about writing your own resume.

Of course, if you have basic writing problems, you should continue to work at conquering them. You may want to study Clear Writing or use Words into Type as a reference. Many other books are also extremely useful.

You will see that your business communications will be greatly improved if you continue to follow the suggestions and principles of Communicating By Letter. (Your readers will be grateful too.) With practice and hard work, your letters can be great.

For Reference

Self-Tests: Previews and Reviews

Preview to Chapter 1

The point of this exercise is for you to determine whether you can paragraph the boxed-in letter effectively. Before you try, however, you will probably need the background information.

Aside from matters of politics, the 1972 Democratic convention had its usual share of behind-the-scene drama. For example, the New York delegates voted unanimously to give their eighty-eight national convention guest passes to the Poor People's Campaign. But minutes after the vote, many delegates regretted their generosity and complained that now they wouldn't have passes for their own families and friends. Reactions from the Poor People were equally swift. One black who had hoped to get a guest pass became so angry that he threatened to vote for President Nixon.

Let's assume here that the New York delegation wanted to apologize by letter for those delegates who refused to give up their passes. Read this apology, and put a Check (✓) on the blank in front of each sentence that you think should actually start a new paragraph:

Dear Friends:

_____ (1) What are politicians? _____ (2) Well, politicians are people who are very used to asking for things. _____ (3) They ask for money, for votes, for support, for attention, for favors, for help--you name it. _____ (4) Today we really wanted to give you something, which of course is a complete reversal for us. _____ (5) We wanted you to have our guest passes.

_____ (6) We were sincere, please believe it.

_____ (7) Then came the phone calls from husbands and wives and friends. _____ (8) We listened to the outraged "You mean I can't have a pass?" _____ (9) What had we done now! (10) And what could we do to right things again except to revert to form and start asking. _____ (11) This time, we asked you to return what we had just given you. _____ (12) Hate us; we deserve it. _____ (13) We're just selfish children. _____ (14) But, please, don't vote for Mr. Nixon!

Compare your paragraphing with the suggestions given below the dashed line.

A new paragraph should start with sentences 4, 7, 12, and 14.

There are other possibilities too. For instance, you may have wanted sentence 1 to stand by itself as an introductory paragraph. In that case, sentence 2 would start a new paragraph. Or you might have wanted to let sentence 9 or sentence 10 start a new paragraph.

How did you do? If you agreed with these suggestions or had a special reason for other paragraphing that you can defend, you will probably need only a quick review of Chapter 1. Otherwise, you should study this chapter carefully.

Review of Chapter 1

Everyone has made at least one bad buy, and has then had the urge to write a letter asking for a refund. Here is the letter one frustrated customer wrote to a snooty men's store.

As you see, this letter wasn't paragraphed. Put a ¶ in front of each sentence that you think should start a new paragraph:

Gentlemen:

_____ (a) I don't know what relief I'll get by writing this letter, but I feel that I must get this matter off my chest anyway. _____ (b) I am referring to my recent purchase of a custom-cut grey suit from your Peachtree Street store. _____ (c) As usual, I picked out a material that I liked, and I returned for a first fitting about seven weeks later. _____ (d) But I was quite surprised to find that the suit was very large--so large, in fact, that the fitter innocently asked if I had lost any weight between fittings. _____ (e) I assured him I hadn't. _____ (f) After much discussion, we discovered that I had been fitted with a size 46 XL suit, although my size is almost exactly a 44 XL. _____ (g) Everyone at the store was most cooperative: "We'll take it in a little here, raise it a little there." _____ (h) (You know the technique.) _____ (i) Over the next months, I made several trips to the store for further fittings. _____ (j) By that time everything possible had been done for that suit, short of remaking it into a size 44. _____ (k) Unhappy but impatient, I took it home. _____ (l) That one was my mistake. _____ (m) Whenever I wore this suit, the comments from my wife and my friends told me that the bad fit was no secret

> to them. _____ (n) What do I want? _____ (o) To be candid, what I would want is to be rid of the suit and also have the $256.80 it cost me.

Check your paragraphing.

Either sentence b or sentence c should start a new paragraph. If you chose to start a new paragraph with sentence b, your reason was probably to highlight sentence a. But if you chose to start a new paragraph with sentence c, your reasoning was probably that sentences a and b are introductory and belong together.

Sentence g should probably start a new paragraph, to signal a change in subject. For the same reason, either sentence k or sentence l should start a new paragraph. Finally, sentence n should start a new paragraph because it introduces a point that the reader should respond to.

If you disagreed with these paragraphing suggestions, review the main principles covered in the chapter. Otherwise, consult the Chapter Guide to see which chapter you want to study next.

Preview to Chapter 2

A. New York City holds many records. One lesser-known yet interesting record is that New York City houses the world's largest collection of Frank Baum books (author of The Wizard of Oz). The collection belongs to a very scholarly gentlemen, Mr. Justin Schiller, who sells his books by appointment only.

Assume that an out-of-town student, Andrea Ferster, has heard of Mr. Schiller, and she wants to set up an appointment when she is in New York to browse through his collection and perhaps buy some books. Read the letter she wrote; then answer the questions that follow.

> Dear Mr. Schiller:
>
> (a) Like you, I am a collector of Oz books, although my collection is much more modest. (b) I would love to browse through your books (maybe buy one or two) when I visit New York this Christmas.

(c) Mainly, I am interested in Oz books that were written by Ruth Plumley Thompson. (d) Although I would prefer first editions, I would settle for any early editions in good condition and with nice illustrations.

(e) Will it be convenient for you to set up an appointment for me on December 22 at about 2:00? (f) Please call me collect at 413-684-3260.

(g) I am also interested in early editions of books by Thornton Burgess. (h) Do you know where in New York I can get some of these?

Sincerely yours,
Andrea Ferster
Andrea Ferster

1. Which sentence(s) give the reader an Orientation?________________

2. Which sentence(s) give necessary Information?________________

3. Which sentence(s) express an Action?________________

---

1. (a), (b); 2. (c), (d), (g); 3. (e), (f), (h).

B. Assume you are I. Cary Cashe, of the Subscription Department of Pick-a-Pocket Magazine, writing to new subscribers--that is, to those who have recently sent in an order for a year's subscription for $5.95. You want to ask each subscriber to approve an enclosed checklist to make sure his name, his address, and the length of his subscription are correct. You have enclosed a pre-addressed envelope so the new subscriber will return it quickly. You also want to ask for payment at the same time, using the gimmick of a free, one-month extension of the subscription if the check for $5.95 is enclosed with the checklist.

Write the letter here:

Dear Subscriber:

Many thanks for your subscription to Pick-a-Pocket magazine. Provided we have all the necessary facts, you should be getting your first issue shortly.

Will you look over the enclosed checklist to see that your name and address are correct, and also the length of your subscription? I have provided a pre-addressed envelope for your corrected or approved checklist.

We also have a special feature of a free one-month extension of the subscription. If you would like this, please enclose your check for $5.95 as payment for the thirteen-month period.

Sincerely,

I. Cary Cashe

I. Cary Cashe

(You should have Oriented your reader to the two requests; you should have given Information about the first one; and you should have asked for two Actions: that they send a checklist and a check as payment.)

How did you do? If all your answers to the questions in part A were correct, and you also wrote a letter that compares favorably with the suggestion for a response to the situation in part B, you can just review the principles and perhaps write a few letters for practice. However, if your answers to the questions in part A were wrong, or if you didn't handle the letter in part B to your satisfaction, you should study the entire chapter carefully.

A third possibility is that you answered some of the questions in part A correctly, but not all. In that case, you can simplify your progress through this chapter by marking the following Work Plan for Chapter 2. Put a checkmark beside those questions you answered correctly so that you can skip or just review those exercises.

Work Plan for Chapter 2

Question	(✓)	Exercise	Topic
A-General		1, 2, 3	General Pattern
A-1		4, 5	Orientation
A-2		6, 7	Information
A-3		8	Action
B		9, 10, 11, 12	Practice

Review of Chapter 2

Read the situation, and then write an Asking letter that will resolve it:

> SITUATION: Steve Johnson, a 45-year-old businessman from Indianapolis, has to be in New York (on business) for the entire month of September. While he's there, he wants to take a cruise up the Hudson. (Years ago, he took a most enjoyable boat ride on the old "Alexander Hamilton," from New York City to Albany, which he is nostalgic about.) He writes to an old business acquaintance, Bud, asking him to come along on a boat ride one Saturday in September. He also asks Bud whether the "Alexander Hamilton" is still around, and whether it still goes to Albany. Since he knows Bud's wife Jo, Steve inquires about her and suggests that they take her along.

Compare your letter with the suggestion. It won't be the same, of course; but it should have Orientation and Information about each request. It should also have two Actions and an Addition.

Dear Bud,

I'd like to combine a little business with pleasure, if you're agreeable. My boss is sending me to New York City for the month of September. Of course, I'll have to work weekdays, but I'm told my weekends will be my own. And I'm determined to take a Hudson River cruise one Saturday or Sunday.

Will you be willing to take a boat ride with me?

Years ago, I went to Albany on the old "Alexander Hamilton," and I'll never forget it. Is she still around, and does she still go all the way up to Albany?

I hope Jo is doing well. Tell her she should come along with us.

Cordially,

Steve Johnsen

Steve Johnsen

If you feel that your letter was satisfactory, continue now to the next chapter you plan to study. If you think you might need some more practice on Asking letters, review the principles and do the writing exercises again.

Preview to Chapter 3

A. Read the letter that follows. It is an answer to an Asking letter.

> Dear Mrs. Payne:
>
> (a) The Brooklyn Museum always welcomes visitors from the local high schools. (b) Our present exhibit of Navajo rugs should be particularly appealing to the girls in your home economics class.
>
> (c) As secretary to Mr. Schuyler, I will be able to make the appointment for you. (d) Either Friday, November 3, at 2:00 p.m. will be satisfactory, or Monday, November 6, at 1:30 p.m. (e) Please let me know which time you prefer. (f) Also let me know how large a group you will bring so I can make the necessary preparations.

(1) Which sentence(s) express(es) the Information?________________

(2) Which sentence(s) express(es) an Orientation?________________

(3) Which sentence(s) express(es) an Action?________________

(4) Which sentence(s) express(es) an Addition?________________

(5) Which sentence(s) probably is the key to the letter?

B. Assuming that a Telling letter follows the same general pattern as an Asking letter, decide which part would be the key to each of these Telling letters: the Orientation, the Information, the Action, or the Addition.

(1) A letter trying to sell an ordinary product that has much competition, like soap:________________

(2) An announcement of a new policy about raises:________________

(3) A letter rejecting a job applicant:________________

(4) A letter to the editor explaining why a mayor is corrupt: __________

(5) A letter trying to sell a most unusual product: __________________

(6) A letter to a department store complaining about an incorrect bill:

____

(7) A letter summarizing the conclusions reached at a meeting:

____

(8) A letter trying to sell a superior product that has much competition, like an English textbook: _____________________________________

(9) A letter apologizing for a billing error: ________________________

C. Assume that you are a real estate agent in Block Island just back from a winter vacation in Florida. You're ready to begin renting summer houses again, and you decide to write a letter to several people who rented from you last year. Write this letter here. Mention that the best houses are always gone by April or May, and that the Blake house is for rent again this year and so is the Ardsley house. There are other houses too. You suggest that anyone interested should call you at 237-4589 for an appointment.

A. (1) c, d (2) a, b (3) e, f (4) None (5) c, d

B. (1) Action (2) Orientation (3) Orientation (4) Information (5) Orientation (6) Orientation (7) Information (8) Information (9) Action

C.

> Dear ____________________
>
> After a most restful vacation in Florida, with nothing more to do than gain ten pounds, I'm beginning to think about summer and Block Island. I hope you are too.
>
> Some marvelous houses will be available this year. Just as an example, the Blake house is for rent, and so is the Ardsley house. But we have many other offerings that are equally choice.
>
> I'd love to show them to you. And now is the time. As you know from other years, the best houses are always gone by April--or May at the latest. You can phone me at 237-4589 for an appointment.

A Work Plan isn't given for this chapter. If your answers weren't satisfactory, you should study the entire chapter, since it is probably the most important part of the book. For that reason, even if your answers were satisfactory, you should at least skim through this chapter.

Review of Chapter 3

New York State has an alimony jail, a place where angry women can banish their former husbands who don't send the monthly alimony payment. Write a letter to the editor protesting this kind of jail and arguing that it should be closed down. Mention that jail is no solution for the man who can't afford to pay his alimony. In fact, while he's in jail he can't earn money. The alimony jail is like a debtor's prison, which this country banned many years ago.

Most people consider New York State one of the most liberal states in the nation. And so it is--at least on most issues.

But did you know that it still has a kind of debtor's prison? This isn't an ordinary kind of debtor's prison, like the ones they had many years ago for people who didn't pay their bills. This is a special debtor's prison, where men are sent if they can't afford to pay their alimony.

Like the debtors of old, however, the poor marriage losers can never pay their bills for alimony or for anything else if they don't have the opportunity to work. And people in jail don't get the opportunity to work.

Let's demand that the State close this outmoded, inhuman institution immediately.

If you feel that your letter was satisfactory, consult the Chapter Guide to see which chapter you want to study next. If you feel your letter was not satisfactory, review Chapter 3 before continuing further.

Preview to Chapter 4

A. Read this letter, and then answer the questions that follow:

> Dear Fred,
>
> (a) Mona tells me your son is a brand-new lawyer. (b) Great! (c) You must be very proud of him.
>
> (d) Let's get together for lunch one day soon. (e) I need a fresh supply of jokes.

(1) Which sentence(s) express(es) the Occasion?____________

(2) Which sentence(s) is the Expression?____________

(3) Which sentence(s) express(es) the Addition?____________

B. Suppose you're a lawyer, and you want to congratulate your opponent who bests you in a difficult case. Which reply would be more appropriate, reply (1) or reply (2)? Explain why.
(1) Congratulations!
(2) Congratulations on winning the Cummings case.

____

____

C. Read this letter that Eileen Flaherty wrote to Nancy Pierce when she failed to win the title of Miss Massachusetts:

> Dear Nancy,
>
> (a) Sorry you didn't win. (b) But remember that you'll always be Miss Massachusetts for the Flaherty family.

(c) Frankly, Nance, I wouldn't compete in this sort of thing if I were you. (d) It must be so punishing to give so much to a contest and then lose it. (e) Besides, you have so much else going for you that you don't need to win beauty contests.

Sincerely,

Eileen Flaherty

Eileen Flaherty

(1) Which sentence(s) would you omit? ______________________

(2) Why? ______________________

____

D. Read this situation, and then write a letter in response to it that contains only the following parts and in the order mentioned: an Occasion, an Expression, and an Addition.

SITUATION: Jo Henley called to say that the husband of a former fellow employee, Marie Dundan, has died. Jo also says that Marie is leaving town to go to live in Miami, with her son and his family. First, she'll have to settle her affairs, however. People in the office would like to see her before she goes. Someone will call her.

____

A. (1), a (2) b, c (3) d, e
B. (1)--He knows why you're congratulating him; there is no need to mention it.
C. (1) c, d, e
(2) They are unnecessary because they sound envious and insincere. They also cloud the first two sentences.
D. (a) An Occasion is the event that inspires the letter. An example here is this: Jo Henley told us about your husband.
(b) An Expression is the response to the Occasion. An example here is this: I am very sorry.
(c) An Addition is an appropriate personal remark. The example here is as follows: Everyone at the office wants to see you before you go to Miami. One of us will call you.

> Dear Marie,
>
> Jo Henley told us about your husband. I am very sorry.
>
> Everyone at the office wants to see you before you go to Miami. One of us will call you.

After you have checked your responses to the Preview, you should mark the Work Plan for Chapter 4. Note that if you answered the questions in part A satisfactorily, you should put a checkmark in the column beside "A." If you answered "B" correctly, you should put a checkmark beside "B." If you don't answer a question correctly, you can leave the column blank. The blanks in the (✓) column will indicate which exercises you need to concentrate on.

If you answered all the questions satisfactorily, you can just review the chapter quickly and write those Building Good Will letters suggested in exercises 6, 7, and 8.

Work Plan For Chapter 4

Question	(✓)	Exercise	Topic
A		1, 2	General Pattern
B		3, 4	Occasion
C		5	Sincere Tone
D		6, 7, 8	Practice

Continue now to Chapter 4, using this Work Plan as your guide.

Review of Chapter 4

Read this situation, and then write an appropriate letter in response, including only the essential letter parts.

> SITUATION: Myra Murray works for a large corporation that the Equal Employment Opportunity Commission (EEOC) has cited for bias against women in management. Shortly after this criticism, Myra is promoted to head the Personnel Department. Her rival for the job, Al Westerly, who is vacationing, heard about her promotion and writes to congratulate her. It is a difficult letter because Al would like to tease her without sounding envious. He wants to end by offering to buy her a drink to celebrate.

Dear Myra,

Congratulations! And better you than anyone else--except me, of course. But I guess that's a lesson to us boys. We can skip vacations now that the girls are on the way up.

Let's have a drink together when I get back to town. My treat.

Sincerely,

Al

Al Westerly

Compare your letter with the suggestion. Your letter should consist of Expression and Addition only. It is not necessary to mention the Occasion here. Now consult the Chapter Guide to see which chapter you want to study next.

Preview to Chapter 5

One of the most serious writing faults is the use of stuffy, overworked expressions. Here is a list of them. Write a replacement for each one; or suggest that the entire expression be dropped.

Overworked Expression	Replacement
1. Due to the fact that	1.
2. As per your letter	2.
3. Herewith	3.
4. For your information	4.
5. We have duly investigated	5.
6. We acknowledge receipt of your letter.	6.
7. Please don't hesitate to call me.	7.
8. We take pleasure in sending you this invitation.	8.
9. Prior to	9.
10. In reference to	10.
11. Permit me to say I was impressed.	11.
12. I trust	12.
13. May we take the liberty to	13.
14. It is the hope of the undersigned	14.
15. In regard to	15.

----

1. Because 2. According to your letter 3. Omit 4. Omit 5. We have investigated 6. Thank you for your letter. 7. Please call me. 8. We are sending you this invitation. 9. Before 10. About 11. I was impressed. 12. I believe 13. May we 14. I hope 15. About

If you missed more than two of these replacements, you should study the chapter thoroughly. Chances are you, like most people, are guilty of some stuffy letter language that you should learn to weed out of your letters.

Review of Chapter 5

Copyedit this stuffy letter to eliminate trite expressions and to make it easy to read:

> It is my pleasure to tell you I have sent you herewith a signed copy of your contract. May I take the liberty of saying that I take utmost pleasure in having you join our staff.
>
> Dr. Baker will be back in town prior to the opening of school. He will be able to advise you of everything in regard to the class load and schedules. He will also be able to answer any questions you may have in reference to your courses. Meanwhile, please don't hesitate to call on me for anything you may need in the way of supplies or information.
>
> It is the hope of the undersigned that you will be very happy at Gant.

~~It is my pleasure to tell you~~ I have sent you ~~herewith~~ a signed copy of your contract *and am happy* ~~. May I take the liberty of saying that I take utmost pleasure in having~~ you *are* join*ing* our staff.

Dr. Baker will be back in town ~~prior to~~ *before* the opening of school. He will be able to *tell* ~~advise~~ you ~~of everything in regard to~~ *about* the class load and schedules. He will also be able to answer any questions you may have ~~in reference to~~ *about* your courses. Meanwhile, please *ask* ~~don't hesitate to call on~~ me for any~~thing you may need in the way of~~ supplies or information *that you need.*

~~It is the~~ *I* hope ~~of the undersigned that~~ you will be very happy at Gant.

If you recognized most of these stuffy expressions and were able to make suitable substitutions, go to the Chapter Guide to see what you should study next. If you didn't recognize and edit out many of these expressions, you should review Chapter 5.

Preview to Chapter 6

A. Revise these sentences to make them more direct:

(1) Your order was taken Monday by Mr. James.

(2) Your signature is required by the boss.

(3) The book was written by Adolph Green and Betty Comden.

(4) The contract was rewritten by the lawyer.

(5) The tenants were notified by the landlord.

B. Revise these sentences to make them less direct:

(1) We expect the training department to explain its techniques.

(2) You didn't enclose a self-addressed envelope.

(3) The company has fired several key men.

(4) The city has suspended its parking rules today.

(5) We make rules so we can break them.

C. Revise these sentences to make them more direct:

(1) There are twelve men ready to go on this.

(2) It is probable that these reports will be ready on time.

(3) It is obvious that an audit is necessary.

(4) It is suggested that we should hire a new production manager.

(5) There is a special accountant to handle this kind of situation.

A. *Mr. James took*

(1) ~~Y~~our order ~~was taken~~ Monday. ~~by Mr. James.~~

The boss requires

(2) ~~Y~~our signature. ~~is required by the boss.~~

wrote the book.

(3) ~~The book was written by~~ Adolph Green and Betty Comden,

The lawyer rewrote

(4) ~~T~~he contract ~~was rewritten by the lawyer.~~

The landlord notified

(5) ~~T~~he tenants. ~~were notified by the landlord.~~

B.

is expected

(1) ~~We expect~~ the training department to explain its techniques.

Your

(2) ~~You didn't enclose a~~ self-addressed envelope *wasn't enclosed.*

(3) ~~The company has fired~~ several key men *have been fired.*

City *are suspended*

(4) ~~The city has suspended its~~ parking rules today.

are made to be broken.

(5) ~~We make~~ rules ~~so we can break them.~~

C.

are

(1) ~~There are~~ twelve men ready to go on this.

probably

(2) ~~It is probable that~~ these reports will be ready on time.

ly,

(3) ~~It is~~ obvious ~~that~~ an audit is necessary.

The *ion is*

(4) ~~It is~~ suggest~~ed~~ that we ~~should~~ hire a new production manager.

s

(5) ~~There is~~ a special accountant ~~to~~ handle this kind of situation.

How did you do? Mark your Work Plan for Chapter 6. If you got everything right, you should skim through the chapter quickly. However, you should carefully read those parts that suggest when to hedge. If you missed some of the revisions, you should study those exercises related to them.

Work Plan for Chapter 6

Question	(✓)	Exercise	Topic
A		1, 2, 3	Changing passives to actives
B		4, 5	Changing actives to passives
C		6, 7, 8, 9, 10	Making sentences more direct by replacing hedges

Review of Chapter 6

A. Revise these sentences to make them more direct:

(1) Your raise was awarded by the general manager.

(2) It is clear that we will have to diversify.

(3) There are three committees acting on that now.

(4) They were considered by the public as being too rigid.

(5) It is hoped that these laws will pass.

B. Revise these sentences to make them less direct:

(1) I have a good rule.

(2) The boss has fired the best secretary.

(3) The people expect him to make another movie soon.

C. Check each situation that you think should hedge:

(1) The subject of an action is not important. _____

(2) Those who are at fault should be named. _____

(3) The subject of an action is obvious. _____

(4) Those who are at fault should not be named. _____

- - - - - - - - - - - - - -

A. *The general manager awarded you*
(1) ~~Y~~our raise. ~~was awarded by the general manager.~~

(2) ~~It is clear that~~ we *clearly* will have to diversify.

(3) ~~There are~~ three committees are acting on that now.

(4) The public ~~They were~~ considered ~~by the public as being~~ them too rigid.

(5) The ~~It is~~ hoped is that these laws will pass.

B. Revise these sentences to make them less direct:

(1) There is ~~I have~~ a good rule.

(2) ~~The boss has fired~~ the best secretary has been fired.

(3) He is ~~The people~~ expected ~~him~~ to make another movie soon.

C. Check each situation that you think should hedge: sentences 1, 3, and 4.

If you got everything right, look over the Chapter Guide to see which part of the book you want to study next. If you made errors, find out what principles you missed, and review these in Chapter 6 before going ahead.

Preview to Chapter 7

A. Use either figure or word style to express the following numbers: write "C" if the number is already expressed correctly.

(1) 50 or 60 children attended._____

(2) It costs 50¢._____

(3) The attendance was 5,000 for the first game but 1,500 for the second._____

(4) Her birthday is the 7th of February._____

(5) He weighs 24 pounds._____

(6) There were 2 for him and 12 against him._____

(7) This is the 2nd time I've been there._____

(8) The house is on 46 5th Avenue._____

(9) As of July 1st, 1973, I go off the payroll._____

(10) 2 clubs were organized._____

B. Divide these words by drawing a vertical line at what is probably the best dividing point. But write "C" if the word cannot be divided.

(1) self-important_____
(2) swept_____
(3) principal_____
(4) crowned_____
(5) blessing_____
(6) prolific_____
(7) squeezing_____
(8) tennis_____
(9) crowed_____
(10) browse_____

C. After the typewriter bell rings, you have ten spaces left for typing on the line. Here are some possible sets of words that could follow. Draw a short vertical line after the last letter you could type in each set before returning the carriage.

```
(1) I hope he will ask
(2) went to the opera
(3) saw a great movie yesterday
(4) bought a stunning dress
```

A. Figure Style

(1) ~~50~~ Fifty or ~~60~~ sixty children attended.
(2) ~~50¢~~ 50 cents
(3) C
(4) C
(5) C
(6) C
(7) ~~2nd~~ second
(8) 46 ~~5th~~ Fifth Avenue
(9) July ~~1st~~ 1, 1973,
(10) ~~2~~ Two clubs

Word Style

(1) ~~50~~ Fifty or ~~60~~ sixty children attended.
(2) ~~50¢~~ 50 cents
(3) ~~5,000~~ five thousand ~~1,500~~ fifteen hundred
(4) ~~7th~~ seventh
(5) C
(6) ~~2~~ two ~~12~~ twelve
(7) ~~2nd~~ second
(8) 46 ~~5th~~ Fifth Avenue
(9) July ~~1st~~ 1, 1973,
(10) ~~2~~ Two clubs

B.
1. self-|important
2. C
3. prin|cipal
4. C
5. bles|sing
6. pro|lific
7. squeez|ing
8. ten|nis
9. C
10. C

C.

(1) I hope he | will ask

(2) went to | the opera

(3) saw a | great movie yesterday

(4) bought a | stunning dress

Study the related sections of Chapter 7 if you made errors in this pretest.

Review of Chapter 7

A. Use either the figure or the word style to express the following numbers. Write "C" if the number is already expressed correctly.

(1) 5 parties a year are enough._____

(2) His birthday is the 16th of August._____

(3) It cost 25¢._____

(4) As of May 3rd, 1972, he hasn't lived here._____

(5) It measures 13 inches high._____

(6) This museum is 16 3rd Avenue._____

(7) I saw 5 frogs and 15 toads._____

B. Divide these words by drawing a vertical line at what is probably the best dividing point. Write "C" if the word cannot be divided.

(1) self-control_____

(2) spelled_____

(3) cornerstone_____

(4) purpose_____

(5) crossed_____

(6) brimming_____

(7) consolation_____

(8) closed_____

C. Draw a short vertical line after the last letter you could type before returning the carriage.

(1) last year's hat was

(2) this year was a

(3) when the recession

(4) four of the boys got

A. Figure style

(1) ~~5~~ Five parties

(2) C

(3) 25~~¢~~ cents

(4) May 3~~rd~~, 1972,

Word Style

(1) ~~5~~ Five parties

(2) ~~16th~~ sixteenth of August

(3) 25~~¢~~ cents

(4) May 3~~rd~~, 1972,

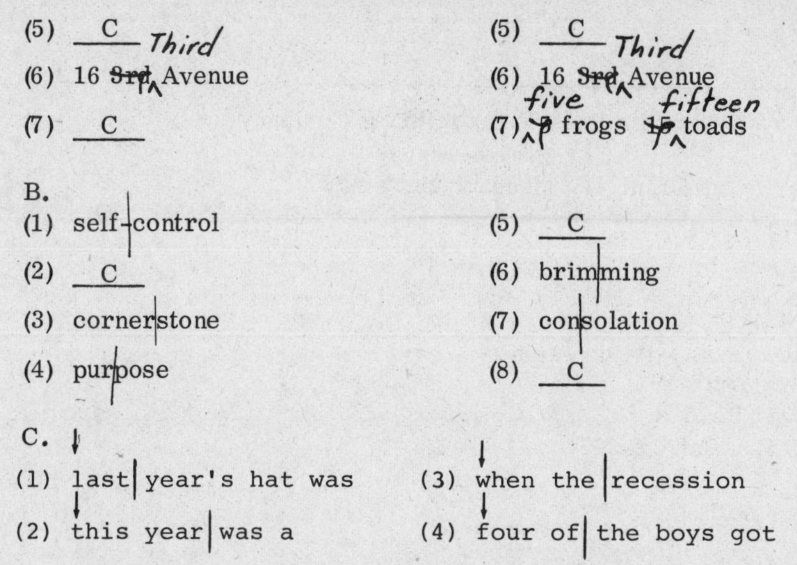

(5) C Third
(6) 16 ~~3rd~~ Avenue
(7) C

(5) C Third
(6) 16 ~~3rd~~ Avenue
(7) five ~~5~~ frogs fifteen ~~15~~ toads

B.
(1) self-|control
(2) C
(3) corner|stone
(4) pur|pose
(5) C
(6) brim|ming
(7) con|solation
(8) C

C.
(1) last| year's hat was
(2) this year| was a
(3) when the |recession
(4) four of| the boys got

Continue now to the Chapter Guide to see what you want to study next.

Preview of Chapter 8

Set up the following information in a letter, using block letter style and mixed punctuation style.

> The letter was written on February 4, 1973, and is from Bill Ferster, sales manager for Plymouth Rock Manufacturing Company, 12 4th Ave., Lincoln, Mass. 40205. He is writing to Donald Faye, a credit manager for Clinton Corporation, 17 Frankfort Rd., Bethesda, Md. 20306. Mr. Ferster doesn't know Mr. Faye. He is sending a copy of this letter to John Endicott, and he is also sending a pamphlet. His secretary, Patricia Courtney, typed the letter for him.

Plymouth Rock Manufacturing Company
12 Fourth Avenue
Lincoln, Massachusetts 40205

February 4, 1973

Mr. Donald Faye, Credit Manager
Clinton Corporation
17 Frankfort Road
Bethesda, Maryland 20306

Dear Mr. Faye:

Sincerely yours,
Plymouth Rock Manufacturing Company

Bill Ferster
Bill Ferster
Sales Manager

BF:pc
Enc.
cc: Mr. John Endicott

You should concentrate on those parts of Chapter 8 that are related to points you have missed in this letter setup.

Review of Chapter 8

Set up the following letter, using semiblock letter style and a mixed punctuation style.

> The letter was written on January 3, 1973, and is from Dr. Thomas Franklyn, a Ph.D. and technical director for Learning Corporation, 47 W. 13th St., New York City 20111. He is writing to Dr. James Flint, president of Teaching Corporation, 27 Rockaway River Rd., Trenton, N.J. 10105. Dr. Franklyn doesn't know Dr. Flint. He is sending a copy of the letter to Dr. Arthur Ross. His secretary, Nancy Sweet, typed the letter for him. Nothing is enclosed.

Learning Corporation
47 West 13 Street
New York, New York 20111

January 3, 1973

Dr. James Flint, President
Teaching Corporation
27 Rockaway River Road
Trenton, New Jersey 10105

Dear Dr. Flint:

Sincerely yours,
Learning Corporation
Thomas Franklyn

Thomas Franklyn, Ph.D.
Technical Director

TF:ns
cc: Dr. Arthur Ross

Hints for Writing Effective Telegrams

Kinds of Telegrams

The regular domestic telegram, most expensive but fastest, is used only when delivery must be made on the same day the message is sent. The minimum charge is for a fifteen-word message, with an additional charge for each extra word. The less-expensive overnight telegram can be sent any time up to midnight for delivery the following morning--usually by the time the business opens. The minimum charge is for one-hundred words, with an additional charge for each extra word. You should use this service when a message is long, when delivery isn't essential on the same day, and when the message will arrive at closing time or close to it.

Counting Words

Since the charge for a telegram is based on the number of chargeable words, you want to save words. These are the conventions Western Union follows:

1. The name and address of the addressee are transmitted free, and so is the signature, including the business signature.

2. A dictionary word is counted as one word regardless of its length. A word not in the dictionary, however, is counted at the rate of one word for each five letters.

3. Common abbreviations typed together with or without periods are counted at the rate of one word for each five letters. Samples are c.o.d. or COD.

4. Standard punctuation marks are not charged for in the message. On the other hand, such words as stop and quote are counted as single words and shouldn't be used in place of punctuation marks.

5. The symbols @ and ¢ cannot be transmitted and must be sent as words.

Cutting Words

When you send a telegram, you of course try to pack as much information as possible into your message. So, a wise practice is to write out the message first, using all the words that seem necessary. From this draft, you can pare the message to the fifteen-word minimum. Here is an example:

> First Draft: I was called to Philadelphia on an urgent matter and I will not be able to see you. I will be back Friday night and will be available every day next week. Please call my secretary to arrange an appointment.

This first draft can be pared as follows:

> Second Draft: Called to Philadelphia urgent matter. Cancel appointment. Available next week. Arrange appointment with my secretary.

There it is, in fifteen words.

Typing the Telegram

Western Union provides free telegraph forms for all types of service. You should always make at least one carbon copy. You would need two additional copies if your office requires you to send a confirmation copy by mail to the addressee and to the accounting department.

The Western Union form on the next page illustrates a completed telegram.

western union **Telegram**

NO. WDS.–CL. OF SVC.	PD. OR COLL.	CASH NO.	CHARGE TO THE ACCOUNT OF	☐ OVER NIGHT TELEGRAM UNLESS BOX ABOVE IS CHECKED THIS MESSAGE WILL BE SENT AS A TELEGRAM
			Sender	

Send the following message, subject to the terms on back hereof, which are hereby agreed to

March 1 19 73

TO Paul Briggs
Coates Company
CARE OF OR APT. NO.

STREET & NO. 4 River Road
TELEPHONE 749-7391

CITY & STATE Cincinnati, Ohio
ZIP CODE 10025

CALLED TO PHILADELPHIA URGENT MATTER. CANCEL
APPOINTMENT. AVAILABLE NEXT WEEK. ARRANGE
APPOINTMENT WITH MY SECRETARY.

John Dodge
Clement Company

SENDER'S TEL. NO. 691-8820
NAME & ADDRESS Clement Company
2 Pelham Avenue
Washington, D.C. 20006

WU 1207 (R 5-69)

Sample Letters

I. ASKING LETTERS

A. Need to Order Goods from a Catalog

> Please send the following items from your (which one) Catalog:
>
> [List of Goods
> Quantity, Item, Price, Catalog Number]
>
> You may charge my account, Account Number ________. (I have enclosed a check for ________.)

B. Need to Order a Single Item

> Please send me an (item).
>
> [All necessary information]
>
> I have enclosed a check for ________.
> (You may charge my account, number ________.)

C. Need to Ask for Some Information

> I would be most grateful for any information you can supply about ________.
>
> [Give reason information is necessary and why you assume that the reader can supply it, if relevant.]
>
> I have enclosed a self-addressed envelope.

D. Need to Ask for a Letter of Reference

I am applying for a job as teacher of English in __________ High School. [Explain what the job is.] It would be a most exciting job.

[Supply any necessary information]

Could you please write me a letter of reference? I have enclosed a self-addressed envelope for your reply.

E. Need to Apply for a Job

I noted your advertisement in [Name of newspaper] for the position of sales manager.

Most of my experience has been in sales, and I enjoy making contacts and talking with people. [Give any other facts writer might give to attract the reader's attention.]

Although I am working right now, I would be able to take some time off if you are interested in meeting me.

F. Need to Make a Reservation

Can you reserve a suite for me [additional information]. I must be able to entertain at least a dozen clients.

I have enclosed a self-addressed envelope for your reply.

G. Need to Extend an Invitation

Monday, July 15, is the firm's birthday, and we would like to celebrate with all of our good friends.

[Information: Time, place]

Can you come? Please phone your answer to my secretary.

H. Need to Make a Sale

I think we have just the line for you this spring. [Mention product.]

[Give information.]

My partner and I plan to be in _____ next month. We will stop by to see you, because we think you will be as excited about the _____ as we are.

I. Need to Announce an Event

We want to tell you about our organization change [announce event], to take effect [date].

[Give information: What happened or will happen, plus relevant details.]

We are certain that these changes will be of great help to the company.

J. Need to Reject a Job Applicant

I am sorry that we don't have a suitable position for you right now.

However, you seem to be extremely well qualified, and I am certain you will find something challenging very soon.

K. Need to Explain Why a Contribution Is Not Given

I know of the marvelous work the [Organization] does. However, I cannot contribute to your fund this year, since I have had [give excuse].

I hope you will have a most successful drive.

L. Need to Make a Complaint

I would like to tell you about an experience I had at your store recently.

[Give Information: Date, what happened.]

I have no wish to make trouble for Marie Donnell. However, I think she is not giving the service your customers expect of you.

M. Need to Make an Adjustment for a Complaint

I am so sorry that you felt you were treated rudely at [name of department store]. I have spoken about this to Marie Donnell, and she assures me that she is deeply sorry if she offended you.

Please use the enclosed pass in the company lunchroom the next time you are in the store. We want you to have pleasant associations with [name of department store].

N. Need to Keep a Record of a Meeting

I thought I should summarize what we covered at the meeting _____, to make certain we really do agree.

[Give Information: Conclusions.]

Of course, please let me know at once if you feel I have misrepresented your position.

III. BUILDING GOOD WILL LETTER

O. Need to Congratulate Someone

> Congratulations. We're all very proud of you.

P. Need to Express Sympathy

> I was deeply sorry to hear of the death of _____. Please express my sympathy to your family.

Q. Need to Remind a Business Acquaintance That You're Still Around

> I thought of you last night when __________ (event, occasion).
>
> We miss you. Any chance that you will get to New York to see us?

Sample Resumes

A

Resume of Clarence Barkan		32 Walso Avenue Bloomfield, New Jersey (201) 272-3749

JOB OBJECTIVE
Credit Supervisor for Johnson Brothers

	EMPLOYMENT
June 1971-present	Worthington Pump 121 Ampere Parkway East Orange, New Jersey I am assistant credit manager for a large firm of 6,000 employees. I have full authority in extension of credit and supplemental handling of a substantial portion of the company's prospective and actual accounts. I supervise 10 members of the credit department in details of credit and work closely with the sales force.
September 1968-June 1971	Charm 120 Wilson Avenue Bloomfield, New Jersey My duties here were similar to those at Worthington except that the firm was much smaller (1,000 employees)
	EDUCATION
1958-1961	Bloomfield High School, Bloomfield New Jersey
1961-1965	Service: USAF. CCA Airways Traffic Control School. Graduated as Traffic Controller
1965-1968	Rutgers University, New Brunswick New Jersey Degree: B.S. in Business Administration. Major: Accounting. Honors: Graduated cum laude. Honorary Business Activities: Fraternity; varsity football.

University of Massachusetts, Amherst, Mass.: Course sponsored by National Credit Foundation

PERSONAL

Married, three children

Volunteer accounting services to civic organizations.

REFERENCES

Available on request

B

Resume of
Barbara Theriot

1410 Commonwealth Avenue
Boston, Mass.
(617) 283-2875

JOB OBJECTIVE
Editor of Science Books, Allyn & Bacon Publishers

Teaching Assignments

Boston Latin
101 Milk Street
Boston, Mass.

I taught science and math for four years. My students entered the science competitions each year. One student won a first prize.

Deerfield Academy
Deerfield, Massachusetts

I taught English and chemistry here for two years. I supervised many exceptional students, and was monitor for the chemistry club.

Writing Assignments
(Freelance)

I wrote five supplementary textbooks on earth sciences published by McGraw Hill Book Company, New York, in 1963.

The Atomic Energy Commission assigned me the task of writing a booklet on nuclear fuel sources, which was published in 1967.

Editorial Assignments

Arthur D. Little, Inc.
Memorial Drive
Cambridge, Mass.

For two years, I was assistant editor of technical reports written by noted researchers at ADL.

Education

Williams College
Williamstown, Massachusetts
Major: Chemistry.
Honors: Graduated magna cum laude.

Professional Organizations

Secretary: Society of Technical Writers and Publishers

References

Available

Blank Outline Forms

OUTLINE FOR AN ASKING LETTER

ORIENTATION:
INFORMATION:
ACTION:
ADDITION:

KEY TO A TELLING LETTER

1. Sales Letter (a) For an unusual product (b) For a competitive but superior product (c) For a competitive but ordinary product	(a) ORIENTATION (b) INFORMATION (c) ACTION
2. Announcement	ORIENTATION
3. Rejection	ORIENTATION
4. Letter for the Record	INFORMATION
5. Complaint, Adjustment, and Explanation (a) Complaint (b) Adjustment (c) Explanation	(a) ORIENTATION (b) ACTION (c) INFORMATION
6. Letter to the Editor	INFORMATION

OUTLINE FOR A SALES LETTER

ADDITION:

ORIENTATION:

INFORMATION:

ACTION:

OUTLINE FOR ALL TELLING LETTERS EXCEPT THE SALES LETTER

ORIENTATION:
INFORMATION:
ACTION:
ADDITION:

OUTLINE FOR A BUILDING GOOD WILL LETTER

OCCASION:
EXPRESSION:
ADDITION:

RESUME

IDENTIFICATION: (Name)	(Address) (Phone)
ORIENTATION: JOB OBJECTIVE	
INFORMATION: (Dates)	EMPLOYMENT MILITARY SERVICE MISCELLANEOUS EMPLOYMENT EDUCATION
ADDITION:	PERSONAL REFERENCES

Table 1: Abbreviations for the States

State	Old Form	New Form	State	Old Form	New Form
Alabama	Ala.	AL	Missouri	Mo.	MO
Alaska	–	AK	Montana	Mont.	MT
Arizona	Ariz.	AZ	Nebraska	Nebr.	NB
Arkansas	Ark.	AR	Nevada	Nev.	NV
California	Calif.	CA	New Hampshire	N.H.	NH
Colorado	Colo.	CO	New Jersey	N.J.	NJ
Connecticut	Conn.	CT	New Mexico	N. Mex.	NM
Delaware	Del.	DE	New York	N.Y.	NY
District of Columbia	D.C.	DC	North Carolina	N.C.	NC
Florida	Fla.	FL	North Dakota	N. Dak.	ND
Georgia	Ga.	GA	Ohio	–	OH
Hawaii	–	HI	Oklahoma	Okla.	OK
Idaho	–	ID	Oregon	Oreg.	OR
Illinois	Ill.	IL	Pennsylvania	Pa.	PA
Indiana	Ind.	IN	Rhode Island	R.I.	RI
Iowa	--	IA	South Carolina	S.C.	SC
Kansas	Kans.	KS	South Dakota	S. Dak.	SD
Kentucky	Ky.	KY	Tennessee	Tenn.	TN
Louisiana	La.	LA	Texas	Tex.	TX
Maine	Me.	ME	Utah	–	UT
Maryland	Md.	MD	Vermont	Vt.	VT
Massachusetts	Mass.	MA	Virginia	Va.	VA
Michigan	Mich.	MI	Washington	Wash.	WA
Minnesota	Minn.	MN	West Virginia	W. Va.	WV
Mississippi	Miss.	MS	Wisconsin	Wis.	WI
			Wyoming	Wyo.	WY

Table 2: Correct Forms for Addressing Dignitaries

Title	Address	Salutation
A. Government Officials 1. The President	The President The White House Washington, DC	Mr. President: Madam President: The President: My dear Mr. President My dear Madam President:
2. The Vice President	The Vice President The United States Senate Washington, DC 20510 OR The Honorable (full name) Vice President of the United States Washington, DC 20501	Sir: Madam: Mr. Vice President: (Madam Vice President:) My dear Mr. Vice President: My dear Madam Vice President:
3. The Chief Justice of the United States	The Chief Justice of the United States Washington, DC 20543 OR The Chief Justice The Supreme Court Washington, DC 20543	Sir: (Madam:) My dear Mr. Chief Justice: My dear Madam Chief Justice:
4. Cabinet Member	The Honorable (full name) Secretary of (department) Washington, DC (ZIP CODE) OR	Sir: (Madam:) Dear Sir: (Dear Madam:) My dear Mr. Secretary: (My dear Madam Secretary:)

Title	Address	Salutation
	The Secretary of (department) Washington, DC (ZIP CODE)	
5. United States Senator	The Honorable (full name) The United States Senate Washington, DC 20510	Sir: (Madam:) Dear Sir: (Dear Madam:) My dear Senator: Dear Senator:
6. United States Congressman (Congresswoman)	The Honorable (full name) House of Representatives Washington, DC 20515 OR The Honorable (full name) Representative in Congress City, State	Sir: (Madam:) Dear Sir: (Dear Madam:) My dear Mr.: (My dear Ms. or Miss or Mrs.____:) Dear Mr.____: (Dear Ms. or Miss or Mrs.____:)
7. Governor of Massachusetts or New Hampshire	His Excellency the Governor (Her Excellency the Governor) of ____________________. State Capital, State	Sir: (Madam:) Dear Sir: (Dear Madam:) My dear Governor: Dear Governor _____:
8. Governors of other States	The Honorable (full name) Governor of ________________ State Capital, State	Sir: (Madam:) Dear Sir: (Dear Madam:) My dear Governor: Dear Governor _____:

Title	Address	Salutation
9. State Senator	The Honorable (full name) The State Senate State Capital, State	Sir: (Madam:) Dear Sir: (Dear Madam:) My dear Senator: Dear Senator _____:
10. State Representatives or Assemblyman	The Honorable (full name) House of Representatives (or The State Assembly) State Capital, State	Sir: (Madam:) Dear Sir: (Dear Madam:) My dear Mr. _____: (My dear Ms. or Miss or Mrs. _____:) Dear Mr. _____: Dear Ms. or Miss or Mrs. _____:
11. Mayor	The Honorable (full name) Mayor of (City)	Sir: (Madam:) Dear Sir: (Dear Madam:) My dear Mr. Mayor: (My dear Madam Mayor:) Dear Mr. Mayor: (Dear Madam Mayor:) Dear Mayor:

Title	Address	Salutation
B. Military Personnel		
1. Army Officers above Rank of Captain	Lieutenant General (full name), USA Address	Sir: (Madam:) Dear Sir: (Dear Madam:) My dear General ______: Dear General ______:
2. Army Officers below Rank of Captain		Dear Sir: (Dear Madam:) My dear Lieutenant ______: Dear Lieutenant _____:
3. Naval Officers above Rank of Commander	Admiral (full name), USA Address	Sir: (Madam:) Dear Sir: (Dear Madam:) My dear Admiral ______: Dear Admiral ______:
4. Naval Officers below Rank of Commander		Dear Sir: (Dear Madam:) My dear Mr. ______: (My dear Madam ______:) Dear Mr. ______: (Dear Madam ______:)
5. Enlisted Men and Women	Sergeant (full name), USA Address Seaman (full name), USN Address	Dear Sir: (Dear Madam:) My dear Sergeant (or Seaman) or Seaman ______: Dear Sergeant (or Seaman _____:)

Title	Address	Salutation
C. Members of the Clergy		
1. The Pope		Your Holiness: Most Holy Father:
2. Cardinal	His Eminence (given name) Cardinal (surname) Address	Your Eminence:
3. Archbishop and Bishop	The Most Reverend (full name) Archbishop (or bishop) of (place) Address	Your Excellency:
4. Monsignor	The Right Reverend Monsignor (full name) Address	Right Reverend Monsignor: Dear Monsignor:
5. Priest	Reverend full name, Initials of Order Address	Reverend Father: Dear Father ______:
6. Mother Superior	The Reverend Mother Superior The Convent of ________________ Address OR Reverend Mother Name, Initials of Order Address	Reverend Mother: Dear Reverend Mother: My dear Reverend Mother_____: Dear Reverend Mother_____:

Title	Address	Salutation
7. Sister	Sister Name, Initials of Order Address	My dear Sister: Dear Sister: My dear Sister ______: Dear Sister ______:
8. Protestant Episcopal Bishop	The Right Reverend (full name) Bishop of (place) Address	Right Reverend and dear Sir: My dear Bishop ______: Dear Bishop ______:
9. Protestant Episcopal Dean	The Very Reverend (full name) Dean of ______________ Address	Very Reverend Sir: My dear Mr. Dean: My dear Dean: Dear Dean ______:
10. Methodist Bishop	The Reverend (full name) Bishop of ______________ Address	Reverend Sir: Dear Sir: My dear Bishop ______: Dear Bishop ______:
11. Clergyman with Doctor's Degree	The Reverend Dr. (full name) Address OR The Reverend (full name) Address	Reverend Sir: Dear Sir: My dear Dr. ______: Dear Dr. ______:

Title	Address	Salutation
12. Clergyman without Doctor's Degree	The Reverend (full name) Address	Reverend Sir: Dear Sir: My dear Mr. ______ Dear Mr. ______
13. Rabbi with Doctor's Degree	Rabbi (full name), D. D. Address OR Dr. (full name) Address	Reverend Sir: Dear Sir: My dear Rabbi (or Dr.) ______: Dear Rabbi (or Dr.) ______:
14. Rabbi without Doctor's Degree	Rabbi (full name) Address OR Reverend (full name) Address	Reverend Sir: Dear Sir: My dear Rabbi ______: Dear Rabbi ______:
D. Education Officials		
1. President of a College or University	(Full name, initials of highest degree) President (name of college) Address	Dear Sir: (Dear Madam:) My dear President ______: Dear Mr. ______:

Title	Address	Salutation
2. Professor	Professor (full name) Department of ________ (name of college) Address OR (Full name, initials of highest degree) Department of ________ (name of college) Address	Dear Sir: (Dear Madam:) My dear Professor (or Dr.) ______: Dear Mr. ______: (Dear Ms. or Miss or Mrs.) ______:
3. Superintendent of Schools	Mr. (or Dr.) (full name) Superintendent of ________ Schools Address	Dear Sir: (Dear Madam:) My dear Mr. ______: (My dear Ms. or Miss or Mrs. ______:) Dear Mr. (or Dr.) ______: (Dear Ms. or Miss or Mrs. ______:)
4. Member of Board of Education	Mr. (full name) (Ms. or Miss or Mrs.) Member (name of city) Board of Education Address	Dear Sir: (Dear Madam:) My dear Mr. ______: (My dear Ms. or Miss or Mrs. ______:) Dear Mr. ______: (Dear Ms. or Miss or Mrs. ______:)

Title	Address	Salutation
5. Principal	Mr. or Dr. (full name) (Ms. or Miss or Mrs.) Principal (name of school) Address	Dear Sir: (Dear Madam:) My dear Mr. ______: (My dear Ms. or Miss or Mrs. ______:) Dear Mr. or Dr. ______: (Dear Ms. or Miss or Mrs. ______:)
6. Teacher	Mr. or Dr. (full name): (Ms. or Miss or Ms. ______:) Name of school Address	Dear Sir: (Dear Madam:) My dear Mr. ______: (My dear Ms. or Miss or Mrs. ______:) Dear Mr. or Dr. ______: (Dear Ms. or Miss or Mrs.:)

Spacing Guide

A. THE BODY OF A LETTER OR A MEMO

Most offices already have standards for setting up a letter. Standards greatly simplify the production since they enable the typist to deliver a neat, balanced draft from rough notes. But if you are typing a letter at home, you have to set up your own standards.

The key words describing the appearance of your finished letter are neat and balanced. A letter looks neat and balanced if it has no obvious erasures or strikeovers, if the right margin is relatively even, if all the different parts of the letter are well-spaced, and if the typing is centered on the page. Chapter 7, Section D, covers what you need to know about keeping the right margin even. The other matters just take patience and experience--and sometimes two or three typings before you get them right. There are, however, some spacing guidelines that will help. The standard-size page is 8 1/2 inches by 11 inches. On most typewriters that page will hold about 50 lines of single-spaced type. But remember that in a letter some of this space is needed for such things as the address and the signature. Even an interoffice memo has space-consuming headings. This means that usually only about 30 lines are available for the body of a one-page letter.

How many words will fit into those 30 lines depends on your typewriter. Most office typewriters use elite type; most home portables use pica type, which is larger. However, spacing also varies. What we want is a guide for estimating the margins, so that we can place the body of the letter most attractively on the page.

Let's roughly classify letters or memos according to the length of the body or message. Assuming 1 1/4-inch margins, we'll say:

(1) a long letter has a body of 20-30 lines;
(2) an average letter has a body of 10-20 lines;
(3) a short letter has a body of up to 10 lines.

Since a short or average letter would look unbalanced with 1 1/4-inch margins, we can use this classification as a guide for estimating the margins for a letter:

Length of letter or memo with 1 1/4-inch margin	Suggested width of line	Suggested width of each margin
Long: 20-30 lines	6 in.	1 1/4 in.
Average: 10-20 lines	5 in.	1 3/4 in.
Short: up to 10 lines	4 in.	2 1/4 in.

If you type a first draft with 1 1/4-inch margins, this guide will help you quickly estimate the best margins for the finished letter. If you prefer to go by word count, simply check how many words fit into each range, and modify the guide accordingly.

B. OTHER PARTS OF A LETTER

After you have determined reasonable margins, you can use the same estimates--length of the message--to determine the spacing of the other parts of the letter. Sample A is the guide for an average letter.

Of course, keep in mind that Sample A is only a guide, and that you may need to make adjustments depending on whether the letter has all possible parts, such as subject and attention line. You will also have to make some adjustments on the spacing in Sample A if the letter is long. Here are some suggestions.

1. Raise the date.
2. Leave only two or three lines between the date and the inside address.
3. Omit the company name.
4. Leave only two blank lines for the writer's signature.
5. Raise the initials one or two lines.

A short letter also requires some adjustments on the spacing suggested in Sample A.

1. Lower the date (from three to five lines).
2. Leave five or six blank lines between the date and the inside address.
3. Leave an extra one and a half lines between the last line of the body and the closing, before and after the salutation, or between the closing and the company line.
4. Leave one and a half blank lines between paragraphs.

Other adjustments are necessary if you write on smaller paper or if you are writing an office memo rather than a letter. For smaller sheets of paper, you can make up a separate spacing guide, keeping the same proportions as for the longer page. And for the office memo, you may follow the spacing suggestions for the body of an ordinary letter. However, you would center this message on the page, so it will look balanced after you have typed the heading.

A letter with a message over 300 words is likely to run to two pages. You may use the same left and right margins for this second page as you used for the first. Beginning on the seventh line from the top of the page, you would type a continuation-page heading: the name of the addressee, the page number, and the date. For example,

Mrs. J.L. Swanson
Page
February 2, 1973

1 3/4 in. Sample A: Spacing for an Average Letter 1 3/4 in.

RETURN ADDRESS
(13 lines from top
of page)

DATE
(3 lines below
Return Address)

INSIDE ADDRESS
(5 lines below Date)

ATTENTION (2 lines below Inside Address)

SALUTATION (2 lines below Attention, or 2 lines below Inside Address)

SUBJECT (2 lines below Salutation)

BODY (2 lines below Subject, or 2 lines below Salutation)

(2)
CLOSING
(2 lines below last line of Body)

COMPANY NAME
(2 lines below Closing

WRITER'S NAME (typewritten)
(4 lines below Company name or
Closing)

INITIALS (2 lines below writer's Name)
ENCLOSURE (next line)
CARBON COPY (next line)

POSTSCRIPT (2 lines below Carbon Copy)

You would then continue typing the message on the third line below the continuation-page heading.

C. THE ENVELOPE

Sample B is a guide for typing a large Number 10 envelope. For a smaller envelope, you would follow these same proportions.

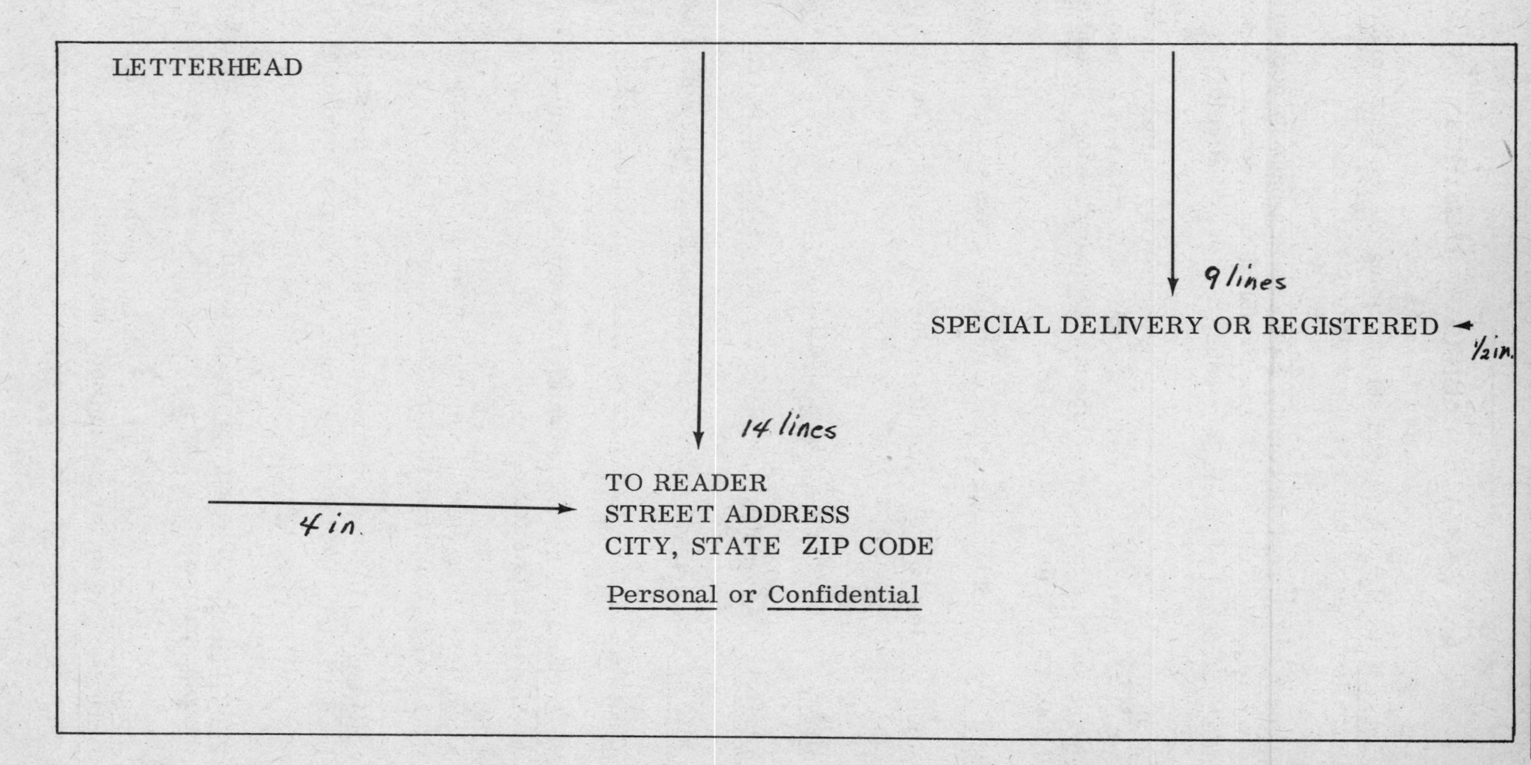
SAMPLE B: SPACING FOR AN ENVELOPE
LETTERHEAD
9 lines
SPECIAL DELIVERY OR REGISTERED
1/2 in.
14 lines
TO READER
STREET ADDRESS
CITY, STATE ZIP CODE
Personal or Confidential
4 in.

Glossary of Selected Business Terms

abstract of title A record summarizing all the deeds or other documents that affect the right to a piece of property.

account The right to conduct business in a bank by depositing a check, a money order, or cash--or by establishing credit; a salesman's customers; a record of business conducted with an individual or a company.

accountant One who keeps the accounts of a company and is responsible for their accuracy. A certified public accountant is someone certified by the state as qualified to check a company's books (accounts) and authorize that they are accurate.

actuary One who calculates insurance risks and premiums.

adjust (in insurance) To determine the amount to be paid in settling a loss covered by an insurance policy.

affiant A person who signs an affidavit.

affidavit A certification that a written statement is true.

affiliate A company that is associated financially with another company.

agent A person or a company acting for someone else.

agreement A mutual consent to the terms of a trade or employment, usually in written form.

allocation The apportionment of goods in short supply so that all can have a share in proportion to their needs.

allowance In finance, a reduction in cost that the seller gives the buyer; in law, a sum in addition to the regular taxable costs awarded by the court.

amortization The gradual reduction of a mortgage or other debt by periodic payments.

annuity (in insurance) The annual or periodic income to the insured, either for life or for a specified long term.

appeal (in law) The act of taking a case to a higher court for a review of the lower court's decision, with the hope that it will be reversed or that the case will be retried.

appraise To set a value on goods, land, or the estate of a deceased person; to estimate a loss.

appreciate To increase in value.

appreciation A rise in value.

arbitration (Often called compulsory arbitration.) Negotiations between management and labor in which both sides agree to abide by the decision of non-partisan arbitrators.

arrival notice An announcement by a transportation company that the goods being shipped have arrived at their destination.

assess To set a value for taxation; to impose a fine.

assets (in accounting) The items on a company's balance sheet, showing the value of its resources at a given date. Fixed or permanent assets are land, building, machinery, or capital stock of another company--all of which can be used repeatedly. Current, liquid, or floating assets are cash or materials that can be used only once. Quick or liquid assets are cash or goods that can be disposed of immediately, without loss.

attachment A court order authorizing property to be seized.

audit A verification of accounts; to make an audit.

backlog The amount of orders yet to be filled.

balance (in bookkeeping) To prepare an accounting of assets and liabilities; the money left in a bank account after all withdrawals.

balance sheet A statement of financial condition, showing current assets and liabilities.

bank discount Interest deducted in advance.

bear One who has a pessimistic attitude toward business, expecting downswings in the stock market.

beneficiary One who will benefit from a gift, trust fund, or insurance money.

bid A possible offer at which goods will be supplied or work done.

bill of lading A certificate drawn up and signed by a transportation company, specifying which goods are being shipped.

binder A sum of money or other valuables that binds parties to a contract.

blue chip A stock considered an especially good investment.

board of directors A group of persons directing the affairs of a company, corporation, or association.

bond A long-term, interest-bearing note given in exchange for a loan to the government or a corporation.

bookkeeper One who keeps the books or accounts of a company, but has a lower status and less training than an accountant.

book value The value of a business described in its account books (as opposed to its market value).

breach of contract A refusal to carry out some or all terms of a contract.

brief A lawyer's statement of his client's case.

broker One who buys or sells for another person on commission.

building and loan association An association of investors whose savings are used to finance home construction and to make loans on improved real estate.

bullion Bars of gold and silver intended for use in coins.

burden A manufacturing overhead.

business cycle A recurrent sequence of business fluctuations, loosely divided into prosperity, crisis, liquidation, depression, and recovery.

capital stock The shares of a corporation.

capital surplus Profits, such as those from the sale of stock above its par value.

carrier A company that transports passengers or freight.

cash flow A bookkeeping account of the current (usually monthly) difference between cash received by a business and cash paid out.

ceiling A minimum wage or rent fixed by the government.

certified check A check signed or stamped by the cashier of the bank as proof that it is valid.

certified copy A copy of a paper certified as being an exact copy of the original on file.

change of venue A change in the place for a court trial.

closed corporation One in which all stock is privately held in only a few hands; a holder usually cannot dispose of this stock without the consent of the other holders.

c.o.d. Short for "cash on delivery," meaning that the goods must be paid for when they are delivered.

codicil An addition to a will that changes some provision of it.

collateral Property that is used as security for a loan.

collective bargaining Negotiations between employers and a committee of their workers and/or union representatives.

commission A percentage or allowance made to a broker or an agent or a salesman.

common stock A stock that doesn't have preferred status in the payment of indebtedness.

complaint (in law) A statement of the cause of a legal action.

comptroller An auditor of a company with the rank of an excecutive.

compulsory arbitration See arbitration.

conditional sale A contract covering goods sold and delivered to a buyer on the condition that he make periodic payments.

condominium A house in which the apartments or dwelling units are individually owned.

consignment A transaction in which the purchase is not final, so that unsold goods may be returned.

contract A witnessed agreement, usually in writing, whose terms can be enforced legally.

cooperative A business organized to occupy real estate or to produce, buy, or sell goods at a common savings because fees and profits to a middleman have been eliminated.

copyright Exclusive rights to publish a creative work.

co-sign To assume joint responsibility for a debt by adding one's signature to another's note.

covenant A promise of some future action, made in contracts and other legal papers.

coverage The amount and type of protection against risks that are agreed to in an insurance policy.

cut (in printing) A zinc etching or a copper or zinc halftone, usually reproducing a picture or hand-lettering.

cutback A reduction in the production schedule; a reduction in salary.

dead stock Unsaleable merchandise.

debenture An IOU that is issued by a business and sold in the same way as a bond. A convertible debenture is a debenture that the holder can convert to common stock.

deed A contract by which real estate passes from one party to another.

default To fail to fulfill a contract or other obligation.

deficit The amount by which expenses exceed income, liabilities exceed assets, or production falls below expectation.

Delaware corporation A corporation certified in the state of Delaware to take advantage of low incorporation fees and tax rates.

deposition Testimony by a witness who cannot appear in court to testify.

depreciation A decline in value, usually as a result of wear, neglect, or exposure.

direct labor and direct expenses Labor and materials that are applied directly to production and vary with its rate.

discount An allowance for cash or a quick payment.

distributor A person or company distributing or marketing goods to consumers.

dividend Money paid to shareholders or depositors as a share of the profits.

dummy A sample of a proposed book or other publication to show its size, format, and sample pages.

dummy corporation An organization set up for some other purpose than to do business.

duty The payment the government demands on goods imported, exported, or consumed.

earnest money A sum of money paid to seal a bargain.

earnings The net of a business, before or after taxes.

elite See pica.

eminent domain The right of the state to pay for and take over a property that is needed for public use.

equity (in real estate) The difference between the value of a property and what the owner owes on it.

escrow Papers or money kept by a responsible party, like a bank, until certain conditions are fulfilled.

feeder A branch line in a railroad, bus, or air transport that connects with the main line.

financial rating Financial information found in a directory like Moody's Manual.

fiscal Relating to finance. A fiscal year is the twelve-month period at the end of which the company determines its financial status.

foreclosure The transfer of property to the person holding the mortgage if the owner defaults on the payments.

franchise Special rights given by a city to the operator of a public conveyance.

futures Contracts for a later delivery of goods, usually purchased in the commodity market on the speculation that these goods will go up in price.

garnishee To take over property or money to satisfy a debt or a claim.

gross As a number, 12 dozen or 144; the sum of all the venues of a business, usually for a quarter of a year.

holding company One that is organized to buy and hold the stock of another company.

income group A classification of people according to their earnings.

index A stock market term that refers to listed price quotations of securities traded on the market and analyzed for trends.

indictment A formal grand jury charge against a person accused of a major crime.

indirect labor Supervisory and other labor not assigned directly to production.

inflation A rise in prices so sharp that incomes fail to keep pace.

injunction A court order restraining a certain action.

interlocutory Intermediate court judgment that is not final or definite.

inventory A record of merchandise on hand and in stock rooms.

investment Money or other property risked with the expectation of profit.

invoice. A bill itemizing delivered goods and their prices.

IOU A paper with the letters "IOU" and a notation of a sum of money, which is a legal debt when it is signed.

kickback An unauthorized payment taken from wages, prices, or fees in return for a special favor.

layout A sketch of an advertisement or booklet used in merchandizing.

libel Any written statement about a person or business that is considered damaging. (Slander is a damaging statement that is made orally.)

liquidate To convert assets into cash.

list price The selling price listed in a catalog.

logotype A trademark or symbol used by a firm in its advertising.

lots (in the stock market) A number of shares traded in. Round lots are in round numbers, like 100 shares; odd lots are in lots under 100.

margin Money deposited with a broker as security on stock purchases.

markdown The lowering of prices, usually to make slow-moving items saleable.

market The range for buying and selling.

market value The price a security brings on the open market.

mark-up An amount added to a wholesale price to cover overhead and profit.

merger A consolidation of two or more companies into one.

mortgage The transfer of rights to property as security for a loan.

net The income of a business after all expenses are subtracted from gross revenues; sometimes stated as "net before taxes" and "net after taxes."

option A right to buy something under certain conditions.

overhead   Fixed expenses of running a business like rent, supervisory salaries, maintenance, or utilities--none assigned to the cost of production.

over-the-counter trading   Trading by private dealers in securities that are not listed on the stock exchange.

par value   The normal or face value of security assigned when it is issued.

patent   The right (not renewable) granted by the government to exclusively produce an invented article or improvement for seventeen years.

petty cash   A cash fund used to make small payments.

photo engraving   A process of reproducing pictures photographically so the printing surface is in relief.

photostat   A document or drawing reproduced by a photographic process

pica   A twelve-point type (has ten characters to the inch) used on a typewriter. Elite type is smaller, with only a ten-point type, meaning twelve characters to the inch.

pilot plant   A business operated to determine what rates should be charged in the industry.

preferred stock   A stock issue that gets preference over common stock in dividends or distribution of assets.

premium (in insurance)   Money paid by the person who is insured.

promissory note   A note promising to pay a debt at a specified time or occasion.

profit and loss statement   A bookkeeping description of the revenues, expenses, and profits (losses) of a business.

promoter   One who initiates the organization of a company or some other business undertaking.

proxy   One whose voting rights are entrusted to another; to act for another person.

public domain   The property rights belonging to the public.

put and call To "put" is to deliver specified stock at a specified price to a buyer. To "call" is to receive on demand specified stock at a specified price from a seller. Both buyer and seller are paid for this service, and the privilege of either buying or selling can be sold to a third party.

receipts The earnings of a business for a given period.

reprint A reproduction of an article or other writing that was already printed.

requisition An order for supplies; to order supplies.

revenues Income from the sales of investments of a business.

royalty A share of the profits that a manufacturer pays to an inventor or an author.

securities Stock certificates, bonds, or other written evidence of indebtedness.

solicit To look for business accounts.

solvency The ability to meet financial obligations.

statute of limitations A law that sets the time limit for legal action to be initiated.

stockpile A reserve supply of essential material.

sell short To sell stock without having it in one's actual possession and with the expectation that its value will go down.

summons A warning to appear in court.

tie-in sale A sale in which the buyer must buy an additional product to the one he wanted to buy originally.

tracer An investigation designed to trace undelivered articles.

trade edition or trade book An edition designed for the general public.

transcript A letter-perfect copy of a document.

trust The holding of property by a responsible party for the good of another person.

turnover The number of times a commodity is sold out within a specified period of time.

volume The amount of business done, usually stated as annual gross revenues.

voucher A receipt or other proof of money paid.

warrant An order for the payment of money or for the delivery of goods or documents.

widow (in printing) A short final line of a paragraph.

zoning Laws governing real estate that set off special areas for special uses.

Index